BEAT
BOREDOM

BEAT
BOREDOM

ENGAGING TUNED-OUT TEENAGERS

MARTHA SEVETSON RUSH

FOREWORD BY
ERIK PALMER

S Stenhouse
PUBLISHERS

PORTLAND, MAINE

Stenhouse Publishers
www.stenhouse.com

Credits
Figures 7.1 and 7.2: Photos by Paula Keller and © MCEE 2015. Used with permission.
Figures 7.3 and 7.4: Photos by Paula Keller and © MCEE 2017. Used with permission.
Figures 8.1–8.3 and Cover Photo: Photos by Risdon Photography for Junior Achievement USA. Used with permission.
Appendix, Ch. 5 Sample 1: "Closing the Gap" by Libby Fleming is reprinted with permission from the Federal Reserve Bank of Minneapolis.
"Osmosis is Serious Business!"
    Copyright held by the National Center for Case Study Teaching in Science (NCCSTS), University at Buffalo, State University of New York. Used with permission. Except as provided by law, this material may not be further reproduced, distributed, transmitted, modified, adapted, performed, displayed, published, or sold in whole or in part, without prior written permission from NCCSTS.
Cover design, interior design, and typesetting: Alessandra S. Turati

Library of Congress Cataloging-in-Publication Data
Names: Rush, Martha, 1967- author.
Title: Beat boredom : engaging tuned-out teenagers / Martha Rush.
Description: Portland, Maine : Stenhouse Publishers, [2017] | Includes bibliographical references.
Identifiers: LCCN 2017027070 (print) | LCCN 2017052018 (ebook) | ISBN
    9781625311504 (ebook) | ISBN 9781625311498 (pbk. : alk. paper)
Subjects: LCSH: Active learning. | Problem-based learning. | Motivation in education. | Education, Secondary--Activity programs.
Classification: LCC LB1027.23 (ebook) | LCC LB1027.23 .R87 2017 (print) | DDC 370.15/4--dc23
    LC record available at https://lccn.loc.gov/2017027070

Manufactured in the United States of America

PRINTED ON 30% PCW
RECYCLED PAPER

24 23 22 21 20 19 18   9 8 7 6 5 4 3 2 1

For Jeff, Ben, and Sam, who support and challenge me every day.

CONTENTS

FOREWORD
by Erik Palmer

"I can't compete with that."

I had that thought when I began teaching. MTV was fairly new, and music videos were very popular. Music, fast montages, beautiful people, amazing dancing, and exotic locations versus my classroom lesson about biomes? I had to accept that sometimes my students would be bored. Don't get me wrong: to hear me tell it, I was an educational, engaging, and entertaining teacher. But I believed that boredom was inevitable, normal, and even occasionally acceptable. Of course, the competition is far greater today. An incredible array of fabulous distractions exists for our students, and all of them offer glitz, stimulation, a fast pace, audio/video, and a quick click to more options. Added to that is the fact that students realize that classrooms do not hold a monopoly on worthwhile learning. You can't compete with what's out there, so why try?

Beat Boredom powerfully answers that question. In an engaging way, Martha Rush lays out the research about how significant the problem of boredom is. To some extent, all of us believe, "Oh, well, that's just what is. Get used to it." Rush points out, however, that boredom is an extremely serious problem. It is more pervasive and more damaging than I realized, for sure. Pressure to cover the material and defaulting into traditional lecture and test mode has made boredom frighteningly common. The result? For all students, learning is diminished because of disinterest. For some students, boredom contributes to poor performance, leading to more disengagement, leading to leaving school. Unfortunately, Rush points out, we seem to be moving in the wrong direction, increasing the amount of boredom. We often give more repetition/skill-and-drill/rote memorization to disengaged and low-performing students. Yet she presents compelling evidence that less "basic skills" train-ing and more engaging activities dramatically improve achievement. I'm convinced: less boredom equals better learning. So what do I do?

Rush adeptly makes clear that no one idea works for every situation, and that teachers don't have to feel as if everything we do is wrong. She simply shares practical ideas that all teachers can find a place for in their classrooms. I don't like theory. I prefer real-life lessons I can put into play tomorrow. Rush lets us peek inside many classrooms, watching excellent teachers implement her ideas. I enjoyed visiting the economics, civics, history, science, psychol-ogy, journalism, technology, English, and other classes in the book, because I love stealing techniques from master teachers. I appreciate Rush's honesty: she knows the demands on all teachers and the time crunch we all feel, and she openly admits that these active-learning strategies take time. But at some point, we have to move past "I covered all of it, and it's not my fault if they didn't get it" to "We never got to the Articles of Confederation, but wow, do they ever understand and love the Bill of Rights!" There is a math problem many of us ignore: is it better to learn 90 percent of most of the curriculum or 30 percent of all of it? Hint: if you covered only half of the content well, students would be way ahead. As Rush tells us, "We lose 70 percent of what we hear in a lecture as soon as we walk out the door." What do you suppose is left by Big Test Time? We have to be much less concerned with "covering it all" and much more concerned with making learning stick. Rush shows how to make that happen.

Rush also avoids gimmicky answers. I worry about fads. "These kids today love games, right? I can compete with that! I'll gamify everything. Here's MitosisMonGO game and my Preposition Crush game!" Rather than suggest what may turn out to be the fad of the moment, *Beat Boredom* shares six solid, all-time winning strategies. As a side note, if you know anything about me, you know I am thrilled that so many strategies involve speaking skills.

Educators grossly underserve our most important language art, speak-ing, but effective oral communication is a key part of many of Rush's ideas. Storytelling and discussion and debate demand strong verbal skills and are an excellent place to teach and showcase speaking. Competitions, authentic tasks, problem-based learning, and simulations often provide opportunities for honing oral communication, as well. Engagement plus better learning plus improved speaking? I'm for it.

I noticed that Rush's active-learning boredom-breaking ideas have many other benefits. In addition to better performance on traditional measures of learning, her strategies involve relationship building, community build-ing, collaboration, research, critical thinking, creative thinking, stronger student-teacher relationships, learning how to deal with defeat, learning how to deal with different opinions, improved self-confidence, improved inquiry skills, and fewer behavioral issues. And Rush understands that students are not the only ones to benefit. All teachers will be energized and engaged, too. Yes, there may be the hard work of changing habits initially, but all of her strategies make teaching more fun. I'm for that, too.

Rush says, "Engaging students with active-learning strategies can have a profound effect. It can change kids' minds about school, open doors to civic engagement and career opportunities, overcome barriers to learning, and close the gap between privileged and disadvantaged students." I believe her. I'm confident that the ideas in *Beat Boredom* will transform your teaching. You know that teacher you remember from school? The one who really made a difference? This book will contribute to your becoming just such a teacher.

ACKNOWLEDGMENTS

Thank you to the many, many people who helped make this book (and this teaching career) possible. First, I want to thank my husband, Jeff, and my sons, Ben and Sam; without their support, this would not have happened. I also owe a huge debt of gratitude to the many teachers who have inspired me, including John Wheeler (my high school journalism teacher), Ann Eastwood and Melissa Dimeo (colleagues who helped me survive my first two years teaching at Wilbur Middle School), Janelle Hallberg (an extraordinary teacher and friend), and the many colorful, brilliant educators who have been colleagues in the Mounds View High School social studies department over the last twenty years.

In addition, I want to thank the Minnesota Council on Economic Education (MCEE), especially Dr. Claudia Parliament and Dr. Curt Anderson, who inspired me to be a more engaging teacher and helped guide me into the world of curriculum writing and teacher training. Also, the many teachers and friends I've meet through MCEE, the Council for Economic Education (CEE), the Minnesota High School Press Association, the College Board, the Transatlantic Outreach Program (TOP), and the University of Pennsylvania GSE Education Entrepreneurship program (Go, Cohort 2!).

A special thank-you to Stenhouse editors Holly Holland, who suggested this book, and Maureen Barbieri, who made it better, and the teachers and former students who gave so generously of their time during my research process. I've been truly fortunate to spend the last twenty years surrounded by curious, passionate, inspiring Mounds View students.

INTRODUCTION: BOREDOM IS A BARRIER

Twenty-five students are gathered in groups around a cluster of black lab tables. Laptop computers are open; small whiteboards, rags, and markers are piled on every available surface. There's a low buzz of voices as students discuss the "Fourth of July Cannon" video they watched the previous night, a brief clip that let them accurately measure the lightning-fast movement of a fired cannonball.

Peter Bohacek speaks over the commotion. "Our goal today is what?" he asks. "Can you create an argument from evidence about whether an object is moving at a constant velocity or not?"

The students quickly get to work scrawling numbers, tables, and graphs on the whiteboards, occasionally stopping to wipe off the ink and start over. Bohacek circles the room and stops to talk with each group. "Where is the data?" he prods one. "Is it going at a constant speed?" he asks another. After a few minutes of asking and answering questions, he announces, "All right, we've got some really, really good work."

He pulls one student's name from a jar of Popsicle sticks, and she and her partner stand to present their results to their classmates. Velocity is constant, they explain, because the cannonball moves the same distance every fraction of a second. Other students then question them about their "uncertainty value," their Y-intercept, the relevance of a constant slope.

"How can you tell if the slope is changing if there is uncertainty?" Bohacek asks. He illustrates t he possibility on his own whiteboard, showing a slightly curved line. "Is it possible the velocity changed? Is it possible there could be some way it wiggled through the uncertainty bars?"

It is possible, the students acknowledge with some dismay. But he draws them back with careful wording: "Within our ability to observe, it is moving at constant velocity."

Bohacek then asks all the students to summarize in their own notes: What have we learned from this? What have we figured out so far? Together, they derive and discuss the equation for velocity—distance over itme—and are ready to move on to acceleration (classroom observation, September 14, 2016).

I visited Peter Bohacek's class at Henry Sibley High School, south of St. Paul, Minnesota, in early autumn, when his students were just embarking on their yearlong physics course. What I found was a collaborative, engaging, and challenging environment. Students discussed and debated; they made mistakes and questioned each other. *Is it going at constant speed? Where are we supposed to put the data? Which one is distance over time?*

While they worked, they talked and laughed and smiled. With Bohacek's expert guidance, they constructed their own understanding of physics principles. They got it. Perhaps more surprising is that I got it, too. Years after struggling through my own high school physics class—never really making sense of all of those equations—I realized that I could still learn these concepts. If only I had had a teacher like him, a teacher who makes physics engaging.

The last time I studied physics was in 1983. What I remember is this: my teacher lectured us in a monotone voice, writing equations on the board while I sat quietly in my rigid wooden seat, trying to take notes and fight off sleep.

In Bohacek's class, every student was engaged. They were noisy and moving around, but they were on task, talking about physics, asking meaningful questions. In my class, as I remember it, nearly everyone was quiet, motionless, and bored.

Most of my high school classes in the early 1980s were like this. I liked many of my teachers personally, and there were a few highlights, like an international relations simulation in World History class, where my friend and I got to be Saudi Arabia. (This was the early '80s, so we spent most of our time threatening to cut off everyone's oil supply.) I also remember staging a talk-show interview with Julius Caesar in AP English Lit, testing our own blood types in AP Biology, and my favorite: writing and designing the high school newspaper, the *Lion*.

Most of my class time, though, was spent sitting still, passively receiving knowledge and hoping I would remember it long enough to take the test.

In physics, I fell asleep so frequently while leaning on my right elbow that I saw a doctor for elbow pain. I remember that more clearly than anything about physics. In freshman biology, I slept through a yearlong series of wildlife filmstrips, and on a few occasions, I remained there, dead to the world, when the bell rang. No one bothered to wake me. In AP US History, I tried to take good notes, but sometimes my pen just trailed off the page or into nonsense. At home later, I would try to decipher the mess.

This makes me sound like a terrible student, but I wasn't. I was considered a good student, top of my class, editor in chief of the newspaper. I passed seven AP tests and went to the University of Michigan on an academic scholarship. I liked learning, and I liked most academic subjects. Reading was probably my favorite hobby, and I did logic puzzles for fun.

I was also well prepared for an academic environment. I grew up in a middle-class family with two parents who were college graduates, in a stable household in a safe neighborhood. I never went to bed hungry, never worried about my parents' finances, never lacked school supplies, never questioned that I would go to college. Aside from dozing off and passing notes to my friends, I behaved myself at school—no truancies, no detentions, no distracting other students or pulling out my Walkman. I was, honestly, terrified at the thought of getting in trouble.

Thanks to all of these factors—my intrinsic motivation, my unwillingness to cause trouble, and my supportive environment—chronic boredom barely impacted my grades, my behavior record, or my future plans. Unfortunately, for too many of our students, this is not the case.

More than thirty years after I graduated, most high school classes are still boring. Eighty percent of classes are still taught by traditional lectures— the same method in use one hundred years ago—and too many adolescents cannot learn that way. This was always the case, but in the 1980s (and earlier) it was just accepted that many teenagers would drop out or age out. Today, we want everyone to graduate. We say we want everyone to be ready for college, technical training, or the workforce. That won't happen if we don't change the way we teach.

Intrinsically motivated students with parental support can thrive—or at least endure—despite chronic boredom, like I did. But they are not every student, and they are not enough. For other adolescents, the kids who really need us to engage their brains and motivate them to learn, boredom is devastating. It's a "huge barrier to entry," according to Dr. Jennifer Vogel-Walcutt, a psychologist who has studied boredom at the neurological level (personal interview, October 16, 2016). In fact, it's the number one reason for dropping out of high school, according to *The Silent Epidemic* (Bridgeland, DiIulio, and Morison 2006, iii). Boredom causes students to lose focus and motivation, and it disconnects them from what we are trying to teach them.

If we want better outcomes for our students, we need to stop seeing boredom as a harmless corollary to schooling or a given, something teenagers will just have to endure, like we did. We must learn to engage our students, so they will have the motivation to learn from us.

WHY WRITE ABOUT BOREDOM?

When I graduated from high school in 1985, I never planned to return. I imagined a career in law or genetics research. In high school, I had fallen in love with journalism—one of my few really interactive classes—and I continued to pursue that as well, spending nearly all my free time in college holed up in the *Michigan Daily* offices. In the end, journalism won out. I majored in political science, hoping it would help me understand current events, and I began reporting for the *Wichita Eagle* in 1989.

That job is what unexpectedly led me back to the classroom. A few years in, I became the lead education reporter, and I started spending my days in schools interviewing teachers, children, parents, and politicians—and trying to make sense of education reform.

The early 1990s fell right in between A Nation at Risk and No Child Left Behind. We were not yet focused on the achievement gap, the Common Core, and the charter school movement. Still, the issues I reported on were much the same as the issues today: *Why do students drop out? Why are we falling behind the world in technical fields? Why are poor and nonwhite students less likely to graduate and go on to college? How can we motivate reluctant learners?*

As I listened to school board members, superintendents, and teachers argue about these issues, meeting after meeting and month after month, I grew increasingly frustrated by my outsider status. If I wanted to understand why American public education wasn't working, I realized, I would have to see it from the inside. I would have to become a classroom teacher. In 1992, I returned to college and earned my teaching license in social studies with an "endorsement" to teach English.

In fall 1994, nine years after my own graduation, I was back in a public school classroom—this time, trying to teach literature and writing to middle school students on the west side of Wichita.

I found that my first students were much like me at age fourteen (or sixteen), but less patient, less forgiving, less interested. When I lectured, their eyes quickly glazed over. They tuned out, distracted themselves, and in some cases refused to do any work at all. Memorably, one young man held his breath until he passed out. (During my student teaching at a different school, a student even started a fire in the back of the room.) I thought I was smart and interesting and had something to offer, but eighth graders could cut me down to size with a smirk or a sideways glance.

What did I really know?, they seemed to wonder. Who did I think I was, trying to make them sit still and listen?

I did a lot of soul-searching those first few years, and there were plenty of tears and after-school conversations with colleagues, where I tried to figure out what I was doing wrong. Should I be stricter? More lenient? Did the kids even respect me? Why did some kids seem like they understood the lessons, then bomb the tests?

It was already my second career, and I didn't want to fail. I knew I had to figure out how to win over my students. I was not going to discipline them into submission; in my mind, that was giving up. Even if I had wanted to, I was not a credible authoritarian. I couldn't even do "strict." Figuring out how to engage them was my only option.

Eventually, I realized I should put myself in the students' shoes. I tried to listen to myself talking and think about how my teenage self would have responded. Was I actually compelling? Or was I just trying to shove irrelevant facts at bored kids? Did I really think my students were going to be engaged by challenging vocabulary words or parts of speech or *My Antonia*, just because I wanted them to be? If not, how would I hook them?

By the time I moved on to teaching high school social studies in Minnesota three years later, I had picked up a few more teaching strategies, like using better, open-ended questions to start discussions and connecting the content to students' lives and experiences. More important, I had learned to take student boredom as useful feedback rather than as a personal insult. I still felt upset when students nodded off or misbehaved, but I empathized with their boredom. I realized that teaching would be an ongoing battle for students' attention, and I would have to work at it if I wanted to win.

CHANGING WHAT WE DO

I wish I could say there was one *aha* moment, one book that made a difference or one professional development workshop that showed me how to deeply engage teenagers. There wasn't. Becoming less boring was hard, and it took a long time. It's still a work in progress—some days I still see the eyes glazing over, and I hate it.

Over the past twenty years, I have tried pretty much everything—jigsaw assignments, "each one, teach one," structured debates, goldfish bowl discussions, review games, History Day competitions, journalism "write-offs," mock trials, field trips, flipped classroom assignments, online discussions, and volunteer activities. Some lessons worked well—like piquing students' interest in Civil Liberties class by telling stories about actual people, like Richard Jewell (wrongly suspected of planting a bomb at the Atlanta Olympics) and Joey Johnson (who went to the Supreme Court to fight for his right to burn the American flag). Others flopped, including lessons that relied way too much on student presentations to teach content.

Over time, I discovered that some strategies were particularly effective: engaging students in discussions about meaty, current topics; running classroom simulations and well-constructed competitions; providing opportunities for creative problem solving; and challenging students to do authentic work, like running a newspaper or starting a business. I knew I was doing better when students started saying things like, "This class goes by so fast" and "Thank you for making Gov interesting—I never cared about it before." I loved it when one student stopped me on a late-night bus leaving the state fair and told me she was excited to vote in her first presidential election because of my class a few years earlier. I also loved when a former student, majoring in economics at a prestigious school, stopped by to tell me I had tricked him into liking economics, that it wasn't nearly as interesting in college. (He's a teacher now.)

I decided to write this book to share what I've learned and what research shows about effective teaching strategies. In the process, I've found that many teachers, like Peter Bohacek, are on a similar journey. Bohacek, who dramatically improved his students' physics performance by using "whiteboarding"—letting students collaboratively solve problems and share their solutions on small whiteboards—is now developing "Direct Measurement Videos" that other teachers can use to enrich their students' understanding.

I also met Kelly Gallagher, a chemistry teacher in Linden, New Jersey, who "hires" her students to be teams of hospital interns, who then spend the entire year of Anatomy and Physiology class testing "patients" for various disorders before presenting diagnoses.

I met Robin Moten, whose "Flex" students in suburban Detroit spend their school days in student-led, open-ended discussions on topics like globalization and humanity. I met Scott Steketee, now a professor at the University of Pennsylvania, who is determined to make math learning visceral and intuitive by creating interactive technology that lets students experience functions.

Despite the amazing work being done in these classrooms, though, we have a long way to go. A lot of research shows that many teachers—in public, private, and charter schools—continue to teach exactly the same way they were taught, or even more rigidly.

When the late Grant Wiggins surveyed thousands of students in 2013–14, he found that the majority of American high school students reported being "bored each day in many classes," "bored most of the day," or "bored all day." Fewer than 5 percent reported that they were "rarely bored during a typical day in classes" (Wiggins 2014). A 2012 Measures of Effective Teaching (MET) study sponsored by the Gates Foundation found that little has changed in classroom instruction since the early 1900s. The researchers watched videos of thousands of teachers, and they rarely observed students engaged in active learning strategies like problem-based learning, questioning strategies, and reasoning (Kane and Staiger 2012, 15).

Sarah Fine, a Harvard graduate student working with Professor Jal Mehta, conducted visits to thirty American schools that were reputed to be models of deeper learning methods. What she found instead was "a grim reality." Even in highly esteemed schools, "most classrooms were spaces to passively sit and listen," she wrote in her essay "A Slow Revolution," published in the *Harvard Educational Review*. "Most work was comprised of tasks that asked students to recall or minimally apply what they had been told" (Fine 2014, 3).

There are many bright spots in American schools, many individual teachers who are challenging the status quo and finding ways to motivate even reluctant learners, but there is tremendous inertia holding us back from a more wholesale change. Changing how we teach is scary and difficult, and it requires patience, training, and support. This kind of change seems even more daunting today, when we add in high-stakes testing and constant pressure on teachers to do more with less.

I hope that in the following pages, I can persuade you that it's worth it. Teaching with high-engagement strategies takes more planning, more thought, and more energy than forcing students to sit still and listen, and sometimes it means pushing back against administrators and other forces, trying to make us do "more of the same." But active learning works much better than passive learning, and it is a lot more enjoyable—not just for the students, but for us.

1

ENGAGE THE STUDENTS WHO NEED IT MOST

Abrahan Muro doesn't remember much about his high school days in Las Vegas, except that he was bored most of the time. When he showed up for English in ninth grade—usually late—he would cruise to the back of the room, sit with his friends, and just try to pass time while the teacher talked (personal interview, October 16, 2016).

> *As I walk in late, the teacher is already giving her lecture. Half the kids have their head down. She was an older lady, couldn't really raise her voice. . . . I'd put my stuff down and either be on the phone or talk amongst my classmates. We didn't really care. At the end of the day, sometimes she would hand out a piece of paper that was my homework, and that was it. . . . She handed us books. We never opened them.*

Now in his twenties and a utility worker, Abrahan says he was a "knuckle-headed hardhead back then" and didn't care about school. His parents, both immigrants, hadn't graduated from high school; it wasn't a priority for him either. His mom wanted him to do well, but she worked ten-hour shifts, and his dad wasn't living at home. No one checked on his homework or pushed him to get good grades.

Abrahan had one class he liked: Automotive.

> *It was hands on, you had a lab. You had a whole space with tools and cars . . . the environment of other kids wanting to learn and do your own work. To me that was cool. That's why I liked it and did well in the class.*

Except for that one hour, Abrahan's high school days were repetitive and dull. He was disengaged, and his motivation was rock-bottom. His report cards were filled with Ds and Fs.

Hannah Erwin, who grew up in the south suburbs of Minneapolis/St. Paul, has much more positive memories of high school, but she had a few boring classes as well—especially ninth-grade Algebra (personal interview, September 16, 2016).

> *The teacher would just stand in front of the room. "Here's this problem." She would show you the problem and then give you a worksheet, and the homework would be written on the board. That was all. . . . My thoughts would wander. I like to draw a lot, so I'd normally have a picture I would be working on, and I would pull it out during class and work on it. . . . It was the same thing every single day. I just stopped—I stopped trying to pay attention.*

Hannah, also in her twenties and studying to be a teacher, did care about school. She knew from a young age—probably first grade, she says—that she would get her diploma and go on to college. She was intrinsically motivated, but if she hadn't been, her mother would have been on her case. The quality of her work slipped when she was bored—but never too much.

The teacher could be dry as a brick, and I would still do the work. But I also felt like I didn't learn the material as well as I possibly could have. I always felt really behind, like I was missing something.

Boredom has no barriers—it isn't limited to certain schools or certain students; it isn't limited by gender, race, ethnicity, IQ, or socioeconomic status. Sixty-six percent of high school students surveyed across the United States say they are bored in class every day. According to one survey, high school juniors are bored 58 percent of the time they are in class (Macklem 2015). Boredom, described as an emotional state, is attracting the attention of psychologists and education researchers, who have linked it to drug use, truancy, delinquency, decreased achievement, and dropout rates. Even the military is studying how boredom interferes with effective learning and training. Psychologist Jennifer Vogel-Walcutt has worked with the US Marine Corps to develop instructional strategies that promote cognitive readiness.

Why do we get bored? Psychologists say boredom serves a purpose. It lets us know when it's time to stop what we're doing and move on to something else. Boredom can even inspire creativity. But most high school students, like Abrahan and Hannah, are not free to move on or do something creative when they get bored. Instead, they are told to sit still, be quiet, pay attention, or face consequences. So they react—either by withdrawing, distracting themselves, or acting out.

The consequences for this misbehavior vary dramatically. Students like Abrahan, who lack intrinsic motivation, strong parental support for education, and a sense of purpose for attending school, are more likely to give up when they are bored. Abrahan barely made it to graduation, after earning all Ds and Fs freshman and sophomore years. In his junior year, an assistant principal took a personal interest in him and helped him make up credits. He took tests to qualify for course credit in Spanish, made up English credits during the school day with the district's online "Academy for Individualized Study" and made up math credits after school. "That's when it started to click," Abrahan says. "Luckily for me."

Students like Hannah are far more likely to persist and earn decent grades in spite of boredom, knowing that college and a good job are on the far horizon. For her, failure was never an option, not even when she was completely tuned out. "I was always a looking-toward-the-future kind of person," she said. "So I thought, 'I have to get a good grade in this class to get a good GPA to get into a good college to get a good job.'"

WHY ARE OUR STUDENTS BORED?

John Eastwood, a psychologist at York University in Toronto, created a website called www.boredomlab.org to share ideas and new research about boredom and how it impacts motivation. We all know what it feels like to be bored, he says, but it's harder to define exactly what boredom is. His definition is this:

> *Boredom is the unfulfilled desire for satisfying activity. It's an unpleasant state that involves difficulty focusing our attention, a sense that time is passing slowly, and feeling tired and lethargic or irritable and restless. (Eastwood 2014)*

We have all experienced boredom, whether in our own high school physics classes, at staff meetings, waiting in line at the Department of Motor Vehicles, waiting for previews to end so our movie will start, or even sitting through a movie we didn't want to see. During action films with too many characters, I inevitably lose the thread of the plot. I have slept right through two *Lord of the Rings* movies (which I went to with my sons)—I was so disconnected from the action and so bored that I literally couldn't prop my eyes open. This is what I think about when I see students nod off.

In her book *Boredom in the Classroom*, Gayle Macklem (2015) explains that boredom can be mild, unpleasant, or in the most severe cases, actually painful. Think of the most boring meeting you've ever been to—and imagine you cannot distract yourself with your phone, computer, papers to grade, or even a colleague to talk to. Researchers at the University of Virginia found that many people—in fact, two-thirds of men—would rather give themselves painful electrical shocks than sit idly like this for just fifteen minutes (Ledford 2014).

Vogel-Walcutt (personal interview, October 16, 2016) said students become bored in class for four major reasons:

- when the work they are doing feels meaningless,

- when activities are abstract or repetitive,

- when students feel confined in their environment, and

- when students have little power or control.

When teenagers are in one of these situations, she said, arousal levels in their brains drop. They struggle to maintain focus and energy levels. Like Abrahan and Hannah, they mentally check out. "It reduces their ability to take in information," Vogel-Walcutt explains. "You just don't have the energy to pay attention." In short, she says, "If a student isn't happy and isn't awake, then he or she isn't learning."

Unfortunately, the four criteria Vogel-Walcutt listed describe the environment in most American high school classrooms. Students file in and take their assigned seats. They are confined and given little control over what happens next. They sit quietly and take notes—an abstract, repetitive activity—while the teacher lectures. Then perhaps they work quietly on reading, practice problems, or worksheets.

You might think this description is dated, or you might blame this situation on No Child Left Behind, the Common Core, and the current high-stakes testing climate. According to Sarah Fine, who traveled the United States in search of engaging, deep-learning classrooms, these trends are not the culprit. Most classrooms were this way before the reform movements of the 1980s, 1990s, and early 2000s, and they remain this way even after waves of reform (personal interview, May 13, 2016).

It's hard to explain why, given so many attempts at change. Fine says she thinks we have a hard time stepping outside of what is familiar and really thinking about how to teach differently. "I have rarely met a teacher who doesn't express a desire to be doing richer work with their students," she says. "I think it's complicated, but I think that for a number of reasons, there's a lack of imagination around what it would look and feel like to do that kind of work. And I think the lack of imagination is due in part to longstanding cycles of how teachers think about teaching. [Teachers] draw on the models they have from when they were students."

There is also a fear that students wouldn't learn in any environment other than a tightly controlled, lecture-based classroom.

According to Fine, "When you're a teacher, you gain a certain level of competency, and doing things differently requires letting go of some of that. Change is hard."

We shouldn't be surprised when our traditional teaching methods result in boredom, lack of engagement, and for many, low achievement. Our brains just aren't made to learn this way.

Although every individual's information processing is slightly different, we all basically learn by attending to new information in our environment (physical, visual, or auditory), processing it in our short-term memory, relating it to information we already know, and filing it away in our long-term memory for future use. If the information isn't novel or interesting—or if it doesn't relate to anything we already know—it will not connect to existing information in our long-term memory.

In Vogel-Walcutt's opinion, when we attempt to learn by memorizing discrete pieces of information from a textbook, blackboard, or PowerPoint, we retain only a portion of the information; novices will remember only the most obvious details. If the information is not stored in long-term memory, we will never be able to retrieve it again.

To get a sense of what it's like to learn discrete, difficult facts, try reading and learning this passage, which comes from the *New England Journal of Medicine*.

> *The investigational vaccine consists of four recombinant dengue vaccine viruses (CYD 1 through 4), each constructed by substituting genes encoding the pre-membrane and envelope proteins of the yellow fever 17D vaccine virus with those from wild-type dengue viruses. These formulations are combined into a single preparation containing 5.0 log10 median cell-culture infectious doses (CCID50) per serotype and are formulated as a powder and solvent (0.4% sodium chloride) for suspension. (Villar, et al. 2015)*

Do you feel confident in your understanding of this procedure? Will you remember it later? These instructions for a vaccine trial probably make perfect sense to the intended audience—researchers or physicians who are interested in this trial and have the requisite vocabulary. They would probably remember them with little effort.

To the rest of us, this passage might as well be talking about DNA sequencing or the speed of light. If we aren't interested or we don't have the appropriate background and prior knowledge, new information is simply lost on us. We might be able to memorize it, but we won't understand.

If we aren't attending to the new information—if you just skipped over the passage, for example (and I'm sure many readers will)—the effect is the same. Think back to Abrahan sitting in his freshman English class, chatting with friends and paying no mind to what the teacher was saying. He was exposed to the information, but he wasn't attending to it, so none of it made its way into his long-term memory. The teacher's words just flowed past him, like a train passing by on another track.

Vogel-Walcutt agrees that when instruction is that disconnected from student engagement, students are unlikely to retain much of the information presented. "Putting [students] in classrooms where they are bored to tears, it's negative training," she says. "We have to understand those chemicals; we have to understand that a brain that isn't primed and ready for learning is only going to be exposed to information. And exposure is not enough."

HOW DOES BOREDOM AFFECT ACHIEVEMENT?

Most teachers feel deeply frustrated when they sense that students are drifting away from a lesson. We teachers are under tremendous pressure to cover a certain amount of material, and when students are playing on their phones, doodling, talking to their friends, or dozing off, we want to get them back on task. We might blame them for being distracted, call out their names, slam a hand on a desk, or sentence them to sit in the corner or hall. Our intentions are good; we want them to pay attention and learn what we are telling them.

But Vogel-Walcutt believes that students actually can't help it when they tune out or grow restless. These are coping mechanisms—essentially, strategies to keep themselves awake. When she was a student, she used to doodle all over the backs of her notebooks, figuring out how she would spend the money if she won the lottery.

Teachers often think that a distracted or disruptive student is just a weak student who is not academically motivated. I've certainly jumped to that conclusion a few times myself. But students themselves say their behavior and motivation vary dramatically from class to class. An engaged student in one class will completely check out in another if the teaching style doesn't give their brain an opportunity to engage.

Marcus Peterson, a young teacher at a Washington, D.C., charter school, enjoyed most of his own high school classes in New York City, especially AP

Biology and AP English. He graduated with a Regents Diploma and college credit. But he remembers clearly how his motivation level changed when he walked into World History. Every day, the teacher would write lengthy notes on the board before class started, then sit behind the desk and lecture at students—with no discussion or activities—for the entire hour (personal interview, August 9, 2016).

> *He was just talking and just telling stuff, and I'm looking at the board and there is just dates, and I'm just copying everything down, and my head just started to hurt. And I was, like, "I don't want to be here." I'm looking at the clock. I look down at my paper and there are just lines and circles. I ended up joking around and laughing with friends at my table, and I actually got in trouble. . . . The teacher made me sit in the corner facing the wall. I just could not take that class.*

Like Hannah Erwin, Marcus never let himself fail a class. But his boredom impacted his effort—and his achievement.

> *At that point, I knew I still had to pass the class, I was going to still pass the class. I also knew that I still wanted to get a good grade, but performing exceedingly well wasn't the top priority. Just get it done. Just get enough done that way, to the point where I was still getting a decent grade in the class.*

Vogel-Walcutt's research has found that boredom accounts for about 25 percent of the variation in student achievement. That is roughly the same variation that occurs due to innate intelligence (Koerth-Baker 2016, 147). The impact of boredom is the same whether students fall asleep, distract themselves, or even skip class entirely. Boredom interferes with school performance as much as anxiety, which is much more widely studied and addressed.

Richard Peckrun, a researcher at the University of Munich, followed 424 university students over an academic year, measuring boredom levels and documenting exam scores. "The team found evidence of a cycle in which boredom begot lower exam results, which resulted in more disengagement from class and higher levels of boredom" (Koerth-Baker 2016, 148). In other words, boredom starts a vicious cycle, which eventually results in some students withdrawing from learning entirely.

WHY IS THE IMPACT MAGNIFIED FOR SOME STUDENTS?

Sola Olateju was one of my students between 2010 and 2014. He was a gregarious teenager who loved discussions, competitions, simulations—anything that could get the adrenaline flowing and feel like a game. He was outspoken, a natural leader, and sometimes a bit of a joker. But when he was forced to sit through a boring class, taking notes on slide after slide for a whole day (or week) without any chance to interact, he checked out. "I might still be writing, but I'm not absorbing well at all," he explains. "To have to sit in a class and just listen without any interaction or minimal interaction, it's just so hard to focus. Especially for people who are hungry to learn" (personal interview, October 26, 2016).

Sola said he cared a lot about grades when he started high school, but eventually he stopped worrying so much. He put more effort into engaging extracurriculars, like football, basketball, and Youth in Government, and less into classwork. "I switched my focus from getting the best grades possible to trying to learn what I could," he says. Despite his reduced focus on grades, his efforts were enough to get him into college, where he is thriving in smaller, more interactive classes.

Every student I surveyed or interviewed in the process of writing this book told similar stories about boredom and disengagement in high school. They talked of hours spent surfing social media, fixing their nails, getting out of class to see the nurse, sleeping, or just focusing their minds on extracurriculars, other classes, or their social lives. "I was literally doing nothing for an hour—sitting there staring at a wall," one student told me. "Often I would kind of tune out and work on other things, either directly or just in thought," another said.

If nearly every student is feeling bored in some classes, and their brains are checked out, we have to wonder why some students are still able to succeed, graduate, go to college, and pursue a career, while others are not. Why was Marcus able to maintain a "decent grade" in a class where he sat joking and laughing with friends? Why was Sola able to focus on extracurriculars and let his mind wander during class without any serious repercussions?

Why do too many other students—nearly half of black, Hispanic, and Native American high school dropouts—report that boredom is what caused them to give up on school altogether (Macklem 2015)? Is it something different about them?

Vogel-Walcutt says some students need "only a fraction of the typical processing speed to pick up everything that's said in class." Others, though, need every step explained, and if they can't stay focused, they won't process enough to understand. In other words, if you are a quick learner, you can afford to be bored.

In addition, home environment makes a huge difference. A teenager growing up in a stable, supportive environment starts each school day with greater available memory capacity, so even when they partly tune out, they are picking up more than a teenager who is preoccupied thinking about a parent's mood, where their next meal is coming from, or where they will sleep that night.

Having a parent who will ask questions and check on grades also makes a huge difference. "If a student lives with a family that values good grades in class, students do better," Vogel-Walcutt says. The PowerPoint notes may still be boring, but the student is now incentivized to try to pay attention in order to avoid trouble.

In short, students who are highly motivated to achieve academically—whether through intrinsic or extrinsic motivation—develop strategies to keep themselves focused enough in class to get by, or they figure out ways to teach themselves the material independently. Fine describes them as middle-class students who are "internalizing the expectations their community and family have around them." The belief that school fundamentally matters and will give you a brighter future can "serve as a kind of fail-safe even when the instruction they're being exposed to isn't particularly interesting to them," she says.

Students who lack that fail-safe are at the greatest risk when our instruction isn't engaging, and these students are often on the wrong side of the achievement gap. Marcus spent one and a half years after college doing development work at a New York City public high school. He worked with seniors in advisory classes and college prep classes, and he saw the problem firsthand. Many of his students saw no purpose to their classes and couldn't stand sitting still listening, so they found ways to escape—by going to the nurse, going to the bathroom, walking out, or getting kicked out. "They would come to my office, just try to find every other reason not to go to class," he says. "They could not stand to be in that class, and to hear the teacher getting on them to get on task was another burden. . . . They found a way to either get kicked out or . . . leave."

The students he worked with weren't impossible to motivate; he often found success when he asked them to discuss real-world issues. "We would have discussions, and they would police each other—'be quiet, we're having a real discussion now.'" In fall 2015, he showed them the video of the Spring Valley incident, where a school resource officer forcibly removed a girl from a South Carolina classroom. After discussing the facts, he asked the students: *Why do you think this happened? When would it be okay for something like this to happen? Could it happen here? Who was most at fault? Tell us why.* Soon, he says, "it turned into them posing questions to the group, and they carried the conversation on."

Later in the year, he asked the students to research potential careers. They had to find the expected and average salaries, required education and background, responsibilities, hard and soft skills, and demand in the field, then prepare a presentation using PowerPoint, a display board, a website, or some other form of presentation. The students dived into the project and asked for his help to make their presentations professional. "They really took pride in their projects, and they took it seriously," he says.

So are the students or the teachers at fault when kids are bored? I think Marcus's experience reveals why this is a false dichotomy. Critics of public education often blame teachers for failing to engage and motivate challenging students, while teachers often blame societal forces beyond their control, forces that make it "impossible" for many disadvantaged students to focus and learn. A more nuanced explanation is that a student's own motivation does play a role in achievement—the students Marcus was helping were quick to give up—but there is room for teachers to affect engagement, motivation, and achievement too.

Consider Figure 1.1.

Figure 1.1

THE INTERSECTION OF INSTRUCTION AND STUDENT MOTIVATION

	Highly engaging, motivating instruction	Moderately engaging, motivating instruction	Boring, unmotivating instruction
Highly motivated, resilient student	1A Success: Engagement and motivation are very high; achievement is very high	2A Success: Engagement and motivation are high; achievement is high	3A Qualified success: Engagement is low; achievement is high
Moderately motivated student	1B Success: Engagement and motivation are high; achievement is high	2B Qualified success: Engagement is moderate; achievement is moderate to high	3B Failure: Engagement is low; achievement is low
Unmotivated, easily discouraged student	1C Qualified success: Engagement is high; achievement is moderate	2C Failure: Engagement is low; achievement is low	3C Failure: Engagement is very low; achievement is very low

The opposite corners of the chart we know to be true. A highly motivated student with a highly engaging teacher (1A) will find academic success, and that's the corner we want for all our students, in all our classrooms. An unmotivated student in a boring classroom (3C), who is not connected to the teacher or the material, will check out and likely drop out, and we will play the blame game.

But there are so many other possible combinations. What will happen when a highly motivated student encounters boring instruction (3A)? This is what happened to Hannah, Marcus, and Sola—yet each survived the class in spite of the teacher.

What interests me is what happens when a highly engaging, motivating teacher encounters less motivated (or unmotivated) students (1C). Can they overcome the deficits of the student's own motivation? I believe they can, at least in many cases. Unfortunately, we seem to be moving in the opposite direction, foisting less engaging strategies on the struggling students who need high engagement the most.

When schools are rated "low-performing" due to student performance on standardized tests, they frequently turn to rigid, memorization-oriented strategies rather than engaging, active-learning strategies. Even within the same school, low-achieving students are more often subjected to rote, lecture-and-drill classes than their higher-achieving peers, under the assumption that they must master "basic skills" before moving on to higher-level thinking.

Sarah Fine saw this over and over in her travels. She observed a classroom in New York City where students who had failed the Regents Examination were handed worksheets with fill-in-the-blank statements about the American Revolution. The teacher "projects the same worksheets on the board, with the answers filled in," she says. "She 'goes over' the content while kids copy it down." In other classrooms, Fine saw students "learn about" cell biology by copying diagrams from their phones onto paper or "learn math" by listening to teachers answering their own questions.

Jeannie Oakes, a professor emeritus of educational equity at UCLA, has written extensively about how low-income and nonwhite children are tracked into less-engaging, less-stimulating classes under the guise of addressing individual needs. Students in higher tracks are given opportunities to "think critically or to solve interesting problems." In lower-track classes, "Their learning tasks were largely restricted to memorization or low-level comprehension"—copying answers or answering the same kinds of questions repeatedly (Oakes 1986, 12).

Fine says she has talked with teachers about this problem, but despite counterexamples showing low-achieving students will do better when given more engaging work, many schools and teachers continue to require students to drill basic facts and concepts, day after day.

"They keep being told they'll be doing more interesting work later, but later never comes," she says.

Eventually, the students despair of ever doing work that matters to them. They give up and, in too many cases, drop out, without ever experiencing the good stuff.

2

SOLUTIONS ARE WITHIN OUR REACH

What is life like in a "state of nature"?
Is it, as Thomas Hobbes said, "nasty, brutish and short"?

What are natural rights, and do we have any "natural responsibilities"?

Are people fundamentally good or bad? Could we peacefully coexist without government?

I don't especially like partisan politics or the nuts and bolts of how government works, but I could talk all day about political philosophy questions. I thought my US Government students would find them intriguing, too. But I was wrong. Try pitching these questions to a classroom of thirty-five seventeen-year-olds, and you get a lot of blank stares.

When I started teaching US Government in 2008, I didn't want to lecture from PowerPoints every day. I wanted to engage my students in open-ended discussions about political philosophy and human rights and why we vote. They responded with questions of their own:

> *Do we have to know this?*

> *Should we write it down?*

> *Will it be on the test?*

I was so disappointed. Why didn't they care? Why didn't they want to think outside the box? Why didn't they see this as an opportunity to do something exciting, outside the norm? I was tempted just to give up and lecture them on Hobbes, Locke, natural rights, and the social contract—let them learn it the way they were used to learning. You don't want to think? Fine, just look at PowerPoints and memorize.

Thankfully, brighter minds at Brown University had developed a lesson plan called *Rethinking the Purpose of Government.* Instead of asking students to consider abstract ideas, which was not effective, this lesson gives them a concrete scenario to consider, called the "Teenage World":

> *Imagine that today, all people over 18 years*
> *old have disappeared. There are no parents to*
> *make rules, no teachers to keep you in school,*
> *no policemen to enforce laws and no government*
> *to make laws. Adult authority and services have*
> *vanished. You are now the oldest people in this*
> *society. You have complete freedom of action—as*
> *well as responsibilities. (The Choices Program*
> *2008–09)*

Given this scenario, students work in small groups to decide what natural rights they believe they have, what problems might arise, and whether they are capable of protecting their own rights—or if they need to work together in some way. This simple simulation prompted my otherwise blasé students to engage in deep discussions about what rights are—*Is education a right? Is health care a right? Do we want a right to bear arms?*—and pushed them to define the "State of Nature" for themselves, without my even introducing the term. It empowered them and made them feel like their voices mattered.

On the second day of the lesson, the students identify common concerns—like how to feed themselves and educate younger children—and contemplate what kind of government, if any, they would create to address these concerns. This lesson is a clever, subtle, almost tricky way to hook students on political theory. It's one of my favorite examples of what can be done when we step outside of lecture mode and let students create their own understanding through collaboration, discussion, and a well-constructed problem. Lessons like this transformed the US Government class from a boring, rote period into a thought-provoking and enjoyable one—at least much of the time.

One of my students from that class later wrote me a letter, which I saved:

> *To be completely honest, before your class I hated anything that had to do with government. It was a class I only took because I was forced to. But in the end, I realized I learned more in your class than I have in any other class. . . . You even encouraged me to take a US Gov class in college by choice. . . . The class was really fun, and you made the last hour of the day go by really fast when usually it's the slowest hour of the day.*

BARRIERS TO CHANGE

Our students are often bored—that's the bad news. The good news is that we can do something about it. Teachers may not get to create the state standards for our curriculum or write the high-stakes tests or determine the length of the school year or decide how the money gets spent, and we certainly cannot change our students' home lives and economic circumstances. But most of us can control our instructional strategies in the classroom. We control what happens between the bells.

Why, then, haven't we changed our instructional practices on a larger scale already? What gets in the way? As Sarah Fine says, we tend to learn our craft from other teachers, especially the teachers who taught us (personal interview, May 13, 2016). Academics call this the "apprenticeship of observation." We watch our own teachers for thirteen years (or seventeen years), and when we start teaching, we default to doing what they did. And what they did, in most cases, was lecture. If our first colleagues embrace the lecture-drill-regurgitate model as well, it's very difficult for any new teacher handed a course outline and textbook to swim upstream and do things differently.

John Saye, a professor of curriculum and teaching at Auburn, worked with thirty-four researchers on a three-year project exploring "authentic pedagogy"—instruction that focuses on higher-order intellectual tasks like inquiry-based learning—in high school social studies classrooms. His group identified the apprenticeship of observation as one of the key barriers to adopting new instructional strategies. "Given the rarity of any sort of inquiry-based instruction in U.S. classrooms, new teachers are unlikely to have experienced models of authentic pedagogy as learners or in their professional lives. . . . Our first challenge is to help teachers gain a vision of powerful teaching and learning" (Saye 2013, 113).

Changing the way we teach isn't just challenging—it is also scary. Imagine a professional baseball player changing his swing or a tennis player changing her serve. You might perform worse before you get better, and there is a chance you will never surpass your previous skill level. Adopting active-learning strategies, like letting students work in small groups to discuss the ground rules for a new society, is a huge change, and the resulting classroom environment may feel out of control.

Instead of sitting in rows listening and taking notes, my students doing "Teenage World" were sprawled all over the floor, even out in the hall. They were talking to each other and straying off topic, and their responses were sometimes silly and immature. I couldn't just leave them to it; I had to circulate and ask questions and help keep them on task, and it was tiring. Sometimes I felt embarrassed when colleagues walked by, like I wasn't doing my job. We're so accustomed to thinking that students are learning only when we are talking at the front of the room—it feels unnatural to teach any other way.

We may also believe we don't have time to implement alternative teaching strategies. We are pressured to cover a lot of content for high-stakes tests, which often focus on low-level factual knowledge (and lots of it). Nothing is quicker than lecture for presenting a large amount of content. If I were lecturing, I could get through Hobbes and Locke in one day rather than two; I could throw in Rousseau as well.

But this perception of efficiency is false. Saying something in front of a group of students one time is not equivalent to *teaching* them—we know that—and it's certainly not the same as saying the students *learned* the material. In my AP Psychology class last fall, when we were working on operational definitions, I asked my students to define *efficiency* in relation to learning. Many of them mistakenly defined efficient learning as "fewer hours studying." It's obvious to us that this is not efficiency—not if it results in less understanding of the subject. I explained to them that *efficiency* means more output per input, either more learning in the same time or the same amount of learning in less time.

We need to evaluate our instructional strategies using the same, more precise standard. We need to calculate the time required for student understanding, not the time required for mere exposure. Using that measure, lecture is far from efficient. Psychology research suggests that we lose 70 percent of what we hear in a lecture as soon as we walk out the door (Brown, Roediger, and McDaniel 2014).

Another barrier to change is our sense of efficacy. We don't want to feel responsible for our students' motivation, but students say we do have a big impact. I surveyed over 750 high school graduates through Survey Monkey in 2016. Ninety percent agreed with the statement "Teachers could make boring classes more engaging by adopting new teaching strategies," and 80 percent said they would have been "much more" or "somewhat more" motivated if their classes had been more engaging.

Research by John Bridgeland, Mary Bruce, and Arya Hariharan found that 69 percent of teachers report "student lack of interest" as a problem in school (2013), yet Macklem notes that it's not standard procedure to consider boredom as a possible cause when students are disengaged. "Certainly, teachers have had students tell them that they are bored in class, but teachers may attribute this emotion to laziness, student anxiety or depression, or to personality variables" (2015, 1).

We must recognize that how we teach powerfully impacts student engagement and learning. We need to think about what our students are experiencing and what they need from us, not just what we want from them.

WHERE TO START

Peter Bohacek, the physics teacher we met in the introduction, told me he spent his first few years teaching exactly the way he had been taught—lecturing while students quietly took notes—even though he had learned other strategies in his teaching program (personal interview, June 1, 2016). He had defaulted to what was familiar and what his more experienced colleagues were doing, and his students seemed to like his classes. His *aha* moment came when he read Richard Hake's (1998) research on the Force Concept Inventory—a test that evaluates the effectiveness of instruction in introductory college physics courses.

In the early 1990s, Hake, a physics professor at Indiana University, analyzed the performance of 6,500 undergraduates in sixty-two different physics courses, identifying which teaching methods were most and least effective (1998). "He looked at to what degree did the instructor use interactive techniques like paired sharing, clickers, interactive computer simulations—basically any instruction technique besides the professor talking and the students listening," Bohacek explains. "What it showed was essentially the very worst teachers who used interactive techniques, their students learned as much or more than the very best lecturers. When I looked at that, I thought, 'OK, if I'm standing in front of my classroom talking, students are not learning as much as they could. Any interactive learning alternative is better.'"

Bohacek stopped lecturing and started "whiteboarding"—letting students collaboratively solve carefully designed problems and share their solutions on whiteboards. He no longer *tells* his students the laws of physics; rather, he presents them with manageable problems that require them to think, challenge themselves, apply what they have already learned, and build their own understanding. The students work with whomever is next to them, talking, sharing, and evaluating ideas. "I really enjoy that process of trying to come up with a way to give an experience that results in the students' understanding," he says. "I walk around the room, never tell them whether it's right or wrong while they are working together. I want the idea of whether it's right or wrong to be something that is a class responsibility after students spend time trying to work it out on their own." When he calls on students to present their findings, it becomes the class's responsibility to correct any errors in understanding. The students are trained to ask each other very specific questions that start with "How did you know to . . ." or "Why did you . . ."—they can't just say, "I don't understand."

When he sees gaps in student knowledge, Bohacek inserts mini-lectures. For example, in one class when his students were analyzing an object moving in two directions (e.g., up and to the right), he noticed that many of them were trying to analyze the combined motion. He stopped the activity and explained to students how much easier it would be if they analyzed the directions separately. Then they resumed their whiteboarding.

This method may take longer than lecturing, but the students master the material more deeply. The change in student performance was dramatic, Bohacek said. Since implementing these interactive techniques, he has seen a 33 percent increase in student learning measured by the gain in their FCI scores, and a 27 percent improvement in AP test scores.

Kelly Gallagher, who teaches chemistry and anatomy/physiology in Linden, New Jersey, was a self-critic from day one (personal interview, May 12, 2016). She never liked high school science, so she was deeply worried about subjecting her students to the same kind of instruction she had endured. When her students were bored or disengaged, she immediately put the blame on herself. In her first year of teaching—"the worst year"—she spent countless hours reading, researching, adapting other people's lessons, and trying to figure out how to engage her students and make them care. She does not lecture or use a textbook (except as a classroom reference), and rather than using typical high school chemistry labs to get students to understand mass or gas laws, she creates labs that are relevant to teenagers' lives. Her students test different types of popcorn and measure the mass of the water that escapes as vapor as it pops. They test gum before and after chewing to see what happens to the mass. "They're, like, 'Oh my God, it's lighter'. . . like, 'Yeah, you swallowed the sugar.' They have no idea that's happening," she says. Her students also test fake vomit and diarrhea—created in her kitchen at home—for protein, glucose, and lipids. "In any class, I don't want to talk for more than ten minutes. I want to give directions, explain my expectations, and then you've got to get busy. It is a lot of fun."

My experience was much like Gallagher's. I never had access to anything like Hake's Force Concept Inventory or his research, but I had found my own high school social studies classes boring. Almost all we did was listen, read, and take notes on hundreds of names and dates we were expected to memorize. There was very little simulation or discussion or opportunity to consider deeper questions. When I started teaching history, I was terrified because I remembered almost none of it. But realizing how little I remembered about American history was instructive—it made me realize that what my teachers had done did not really work.

Creating and finding more effective instructional strategies has been a long process, with a great deal of experimentation, and it's still a work in progress. In every course, the process starts over again, and in the past twenty-three years I have taught English, Newspaper Production (journalism), Economics, Psychology, US History, US Government, Civil Liberties, AP Macroeconomics, AP Microeconomics, and AP Psychology. Making an elective, regular-level civil liberties course engaging is not the same challenge as making journalism or economics engaging. Civil liberties lends itself to case studies and journalism is naturally hands-on and engaging, while economics is notorious for being one of the most boring, lecture-oriented courses at most schools.

In US Government class, after the success of "Teenage World," I decided to shift my focus from the lists of vocabulary terms in the state standards and the countless obscure facts in the textbook (remember the cloture rule?) to broader issues. I decided that I had just two goals: I wanted my students to understand how the system worked, and I wanted them to care about the political issues facing this country. I wanted every one of them to become a voting, letter-writing, protesting, active, empowered citizen, and I eliminated anything that didn't relate to that overriding theme.

Instead of listening to me lecture and memorizing facts, they practiced writing letters to Congress, organizing mock political parties, and reenacting Supreme Court cases, like *Safford v. Redding* (2009), a case dealing with search and seizure of a student. My students did not learn every fact in the textbook, but they were enraged that a school would strip-search a thirteen-year-old girl to see if she had ibuprofen—and they got engaged and excited about the political system. "How could the school do that?" they asked. "Don't they need a warrant?" "Who makes these laws?"

A CALL TO ACTION

I recently told a group of high school teachers attending a workshop that I was writing a book on how active-learning strategies can beat boredom. One of the teachers immediately responded, "Why? We put up with being bored; why can't they?"

It's a serious question. We did make it through, and we learned something from all of those lectures, worksheets, and Scantron tests. Maybe we even learned a valuable kind of discipline and persistence. But think about what that question implies: Do we want to treat high school education as an endurance test, something to be suffered through? Or do we want high school to be an opportunity for genuine learning and growth? Do we like lecturing to a zoned-out audience and blaming them when they don't remember? More than we'd like to see our students deeply engaged in a small-group discussion? And are we satisfied with a system that works for only some of our students, the ones who are already intrinsically or extrinsically motivated?

I believe we can no longer afford an education system like this. The world outside school has changed dramatically in the past few decades, and we cannot ignore the implications. First of all, we know we need to motivate all of our students today to meet meaningful academic standards and complete high school. Our society and world face complex issues—like how to provide water, food, and health care for a growing population—that require informed citizens who can think critically and innovate solutions. We need to develop thoughtful adults who can understand diverse perspectives, communicate their ideas, and work collaboratively. We also need adults who can solve problems and manage technology. In 1985, when I graduated from high school, American manufacturing was already in decline, but there were still 18 million manufacturing jobs in the United States—jobs like working on auto assembly lines or producing textiles, computers, or furniture. In 2014, there were just 12.3 million manufacturing jobs, and many of those required high-tech skills, like operating robots. The skills our students need to be capable citizens are far more sophisticated today than they were just thirty years ago.

Second, the world outside of school has grown increasingly stimulating and easily accessible. When I was bored in school, I would write notes to my friends, daydream about weekend plans, and fall asleep propped up by my right elbow. Students today have a world of enticing distractions literally right at their fingertips, on their phones or mobile devices. Forget about passing notes—students can Snapchat their friends, buy concert tickets, order new shoes, or even watch YouTube cat videos during class—if they are sneaky or their teacher is not constantly monitoring them.

Nicholas Carr, who has written extensively about the impact of the Internet on our brains, says the lure of electronic media is almost irresistible today. "The Net commands our attention with far greater insistency than our television or radio or morning newspaper ever did. . . . Today's teenagers typically send or receive a message every few minutes throughout their waking hours" (Carr 2010, 117–118). Bored students can easily pump up dopamine levels in their brains by using social media, meaning mental escape is no longer a last resort but an attractive alternative to paying attention in class. We simply must work harder to get the same level of attention from students today.

Michael Corso, the chief academic officer for the Quaglia Institute, and his colleagues studied how engagement works in the high school classroom—and why it is so low. Levels of engagement drop as students progress from elementary to middle and high school, he argues. One reason is that schools no longer corner the market on "from-whom-and-where-you-can-learn-things," which used to be enough to engage many curious adolescents. "With increasing mobile access to social networking, gaming, TV, music, and movies, the entire culture seems to be competing for students' attention and inviting their engagement. And unlike teachers and schools, those who make a sizable profit from children's rapt attention can devote seemingly limitless resources to obtain it" (Corso et al. 2013, 59).

A third reason we must change is that we are moving in the wrong direction; school is actually more lecture-oriented today than it was in the past. We've made it harder for less motivated students to find oases of engagement during the school day. Remember what Abrahan Muro said about his automotive class, the one class he found engaging? "It was hands on, you had a lab . . . the environment of other kids wanting to learn" (personal interview, September 13, 2016). At my high school in Minnesota, he would not have had that option. Like many college-prep schools, we no longer offer vocational technical courses. Nationwide, high school students are spending less and less time in hands-on learning environments. In 1966, 5.9 percent of American public secondary teachers were teaching home economics; 5.1 percent were teaching industrial arts; 4.6 percent were teaching music; 1.6 percent were teaching agriculture. Over 17 percent of teaching time was spent on these hands-on, nonlecture subjects, not even including physical education. By 2001, about 6 percent of public high school teachers were teaching these subjects (Werhan 2006, 22). I am not advocating that we offer more of these specific courses, but that we implement the interactive teaching strategies that make these courses engaging to students.

Fourth, we know a lot more about the brain and cognition than we used to. Even when teachers are gifted lecturers, student attention begins to fade after about fifteen minutes (Stuart and Rutherford 1978). As I noted earlier, students then forget 70 percent of what they did hear. Henry Roediger and Mark McDaniel, the cognitive scientists who collaborated with author Peter Brown to write *Make It Stick: The Science of Successful Learning*, explain that learning is deeply misunderstood. People falsely believe that you can learn something quickly with repetition, that easier and faster learning is preferable to slow and difficult learning, and that single-minded focus on a subject (cramming) will bring results. In fact, "You learn better when you wrestle with new problems before being shown the solution, rather than the other way around" (Brown, Roediger, and McDaniel 2014, 226).

For example, a teacher can tell a student how exchange rates work (1 dollar = 8 pesos) and give them practice problems (How many pesos will 3 dollars buy?). But without context or deep thought, this knowledge won't stick. Students will develop a deeper understanding if they participate in a simulation, where they have to figure out for themselves how to exchange currencies to buy goods they want in a foreign market.

Finally, our traditional teaching methods no longer align with the skills we want students to have. If all we wanted were students who could recall facts and dates, follow instructions, summarize something they've read, and apply mathematical formulas, traditional methods of instruction might be able to meet those goals, at least with motivated students. But many business, political, and educational leaders are in agreement that students today need what are called 21st century skills—which include creative problem solving, communication, collaboration, media literacy, technology skills, and cross-cultural skills. Listening to lectures and answering multiple-choice test questions does too little to build these skills.

LET'S GET STARTED

The remaining chapters of this book are dedicated to sharing and explaining six active-learning strategies—instructional techniques that can combat boredom and improve student engagement, motivation, and achievement in any high school classroom. But this is not a simple "how-to" guide. Creating a more engaging classroom is a challenging task. It requires time, dedication, imagination, a willingness to take risks, and a willingness to give up control. It requires an open mind and also healthy skepticism—even toward this book. (You can find a summary of some of the academic research supporting these six strategies in Appendix A online at sten.pub/beatboredom.)

Not every active-learning strategy is appropriate for every content area or classroom. Not every active lesson will work, and not everything that claims to be "active learning" is worth the time. Even defining active learning is challenging, so I will try to define it through examples. I strongly believe that moving away from traditional teaching strategies will pay off for all of our students, but I'm not going to make it sound simple, and there are pitfalls to beware:

1. Engagement is necessary, but it is not a sufficient condition for learning. The key isn't simply engagement but engagement *with purpose*. Anyone could get students to pay attention by juggling, handing out money, running a karaoke session, or letting students gripe about unfair school policies all hour. We need to use strategies for engage-

ment that draw adolescents into meaningful, rigorous learning tasks. That's a lot more challenging than designing fun activities to make them "like" school. Practice skepticism and hold every lesson to a high standard.

2. Do not assume technology is the answer. I will suggest ways to integrate technology into active learning, and in some cases technology offers incredible opportunities, but technology alone is not the point. When asked whether frequent use of technology was a key to engagement, only 11 percent of the students I surveyed said that it was. High school students are not necessarily engaged because we ask them to use an iPad instead of a notebook, and programs that drill students on basic concepts and vocabulary are no more interesting on the computer than they were on paper.

3. Do not swing from one extreme to another. Education is about 21st century skills, but it is not *only* about 21st century skills. We can find time in our busy school schedules for high-engagement activities like simulations, discussions, and Problem-Based Learning without giving up necessary content, such as which nations were World War II allies or how to measure acceleration.

4. Beware of false dichotomies. As I noted when introducing the table in Figure 1.1, it's very tempting with a problem like student engagement to point fingers: "it's the student's fault" or "it's the teacher's fault." The best students can learn from almost anyone, and the best teachers can teach almost anyone. Our challenge is in the gray areas. The more we can do to engage and motivate more of our students, the better our results will be, even if we can't motivate every single one. Similarly, it is tempting to set up a false dichotomy between lecture and active-learning strategies. It is easy to say, "I can't use discussion in my class every day" without acknowledging that we can use it sometimes, or more often than we currently do. Researchers found that open discussion averages just 1.7 minutes per every 60 minutes of class time in english/language arts classrooms. We can do better than that without making the extreme move to "all discussion all the time."

5.   Learning to use active-learning strategies effectively in the class-
     room requires training, practice, and in some cases, even immersion
     for teachers. Reading about a simulation online (or in this book) is
     not nearly as effective in participating in one. I never would have
     implemented a simulation like *Econoland* (described in Chapter 6)
     if I hadn't participated in it during a workshop. I never would have
     understood how to help students start businesses or publish a news-
     paper if I hadn't first observed experts, like my own high school jour-
     nalism teacher. Now that I've been in Peter Bohacek's classroom,
     I've started using his whiteboarding strategies with my AP Macro-
     economics students. We have to learn from each other.

STORYTELLING:
GIVE STUDENTS SOMEONE
(OR SOMETHING) TO
CARE ABOUT

Tom was a new resident on his first shift at St. John's Regional Hospital. After several hours of checking vital signs and dealing with standard aches and pains, his first trauma patient arrived. The EMT recited the vital signs as Tom and the attending physician, Dr. Greene, pushed the gurney into the trauma room: "eighteen-year-old male, gunshot wound to the right abdomen, heart rate 92, respiratory rate 22, blood pressure 95/65, no loss of consciousness."

Once inside the trauma room, Dr. Greene began his initial assessment of the patient while Tom organized supplies he knew would be needed. He attached a pulse-ox monitor to the patient's index finger so Dr. Greene could keep an eye on the O2 levels in the patient's blood, and he inserted a Foley catheter so the patient's urine output could be collected and monitored.

As he finished his initial duties, Tom heard Dr. Greene say, "It looks like the bullet missed the liver and kidney, but it may have severed an artery. That's probably why his BP is a bit low. Tom, grab a liter of saline and start a fast IV drip . . . we need to increase his blood volume."

Tom grabbed one of the fluid-filled bags from the nearby shelf, attached a 12-gauge IV needle to the plastic tubing, and gently slipped the needle into the patient's antecubital vein. He then hung the plastic bag on the IV stand and let the fluid flow down the tubing and into the patient's vein.

The reaction was quick and violent. The patient's heart rate began to skyrocket, and Tom heard Dr. Greene shouting, "His O2 saturation is falling! Pulse is quickening! What is going on with this guy?!" Tom froze in place. He heard Dr. Greene continue, "Flatline! We've lost a pulse. . . . Tom, get the crash cart, we need to shock this guy to get his heart going again!"

Tom got over his initial shock and did as Dr. Greene had ordered. He then started CPR as Dr. Greene readied the cardiac defibrillator to shock the patient. They continued to alternate between CPR and defibrillation for almost an hour, but to no avail. As Dr. Greene announced the time of death, Tom felt a sickening feeling in the pit of his stomach. He couldn't believe he had lost his first trauma patient.

Then Tom noticed that the fluid in the Foley catheter bag was bright red. "Dr. Greene, there's hemoglobin in the Foley bag," he said.

"How could that be?" responded Dr. Greene.

Tom began to walk back through his steps, trying to think of anything that could have caused the hemoglobinuria. His mounting fear turned to outright terror as he looked at the now empty bag on the IV stand. Its label didn't read "Saline," but rather "Distilled Water." He looked at Dr. Greene, his heart quickly sinking, and said, "I think I may have killed the patient" (Nash 2008).

Jen Nippert and Eric Friberg, biology teachers at Henry Sibley High School in Minnesota, use this story to introduce their tenth-grade students to diffusion and osmosis (personal interviews, September 14, 2016).

"For nineteen years, the kids never got it," Nippert said.

She came across the story at a conference, made a few changes to make it local, and started using it in class. "Instead of hooking up saline, they put in distilled water, and he ends up dying," Nippert said. "That would never happen. But the students buy in to these little things, and they learn these concepts because we've made it emotionally charged for them."

Stories like this are not just emotionally charged—they are virtual gateways to the human brain. Listening to a data-filled lecture activates just two parts of your brain associated with language: Wernicke's Area and Broca's Area. Listening to a story activates six additional brain areas—the visual cortex, olfactory cortex, auditory cortex, motor cortex, sensory cortex, and cerebellum—as you visualize and emotionally connect to the events (Porter 2016). The ER mistake narrative piques students' attention; it makes them wonder: *Why would distilled water kill the patient, but saline doesn't?* (The answer has to do with osmosis and maintaining osmotic pressure between the body's cells and fluids. Distilled water has lower osmotic pressure, so the water would rush into the red blood cells and pop them.)

The result is a dramatic difference in student attention, focus, engagement, and learning. Sibley's biology students outperform schools with similar demographics by twenty points on the state science exam each spring. While storytelling is not these teachers' only important strategy, it plays a key role in engaging their students.

WHAT IS STORYTELLING?

Teaching with stories may at first seem like just another name for lecture, but effective storytelling is far from the bulleted, disjointed, often boring notes in a PowerPoint. Storytelling involves a plot—a beginning, middle, and end. Stories involve people and action, not lists of facts, dates, or data. They also involve conflict and resolution.

Here's what happens: When we listen to a story and the tension builds, cortisol floods our brains, creating an "oh no" response, and we feel stressed. *Is the patient going to die? What went wrong? Will the new doctor lose his job? What if I did that?* When we get to the end—in this case, realizing it is a fictional story and would probably never happen—we feel relief. The oxytocin flows instead. The details remain memorable, easy to access even years later, unlike the discrete and forgettable facts of a lecture (Porter 2016).

Like most people, I enjoy hearing a well-told story; I know my students do, too. Their body language changes when they are listening to a funny or suspenseful story. They look up, scoot forward in their seats, smile, and listen attentively. It's fun to share stories because I can actually see and feel their engagement. Still, for many years I didn't realize how critical storytelling is for engaging high school students.

Psychologists who have studied storytelling say stories are fundamental to ordering our life experiences in a meaningful way. Roger Schank of Northwestern and Robert Abelson of Yale, leaders in the field of social cognition, proposed more than twenty years ago that stories are the building blocks of all memory, knowledge, and social communication. "Storytelling is not something we just happen to do. It is something we virtually have to do if we want to remember anything at all" (Schank and Abelson 1995).

Craig Roney, an education professor at Wayne State University, explained that oral storytelling is "one of the most powerful forms of art/communication known to humans." When we tell stories aloud using vocalization, body language, and facial expression, the story becomes "interactive, immediate, and very personal—a negotiation between this teller and this audience at this time and in this place, never to be duplicated in precisely the same way again" (Roney 1996 7–9).

This is a powerful tool for teachers to engage students. We can use it by building up our own collection of stories, encouraging students to share stories with their classmates, and making storytelling part of our work together.

Steve Rubino, who taught history for twenty-three years in Chamblee, Georgia, made interactive stories central to his instruction, rejecting the typical history class focus on dates, events, and names (personal interview, June 9, 2016).

"I actually had a rocking chair in my classroom," Rubino told me. As he would rock and tell stories, he says, "I'm engaging them, asking them questions like, 'What do you think happened next?' or 'What would you do if you're Benedict Arnold?' or whatever the case may be. Trying to get them to actually engage their brain in the story . . . I tell them they have to think like they were actually there. 'What would you do?' They get the sense that history is a little more personal than they thought."

That kind of storytelling helps students by sharing new information through a familiar narrative structure, which our brains are trained to follow from early childhood. Thomas Newkirk, the author of *Minds Made for Stories*, explains why we need narrative storytelling to help us make sense of all kinds of texts, even history and science textbooks. "Photosynthesis is a story; climate change is a story; cancer is a story, with antecedents and consequences," he writes. "To the extent these phenomena can be told as stories, readers will have a better chance of taking in the information" (Newkirk 2014, 11).

Newkirk is addressing reading and writing, but the same holds true for talking and listening. We need stories to make sense of what we hear—and what we see on the screen—as well. That's why we can watch a movie like *The Big Short* and suddenly understand the housing crisis (and not nod off), while we couldn't easily make sense of the same information presented as a time line.

We can use a story like the ER mistake narrative as the introduction to a lesson, the premise for a discussion or inquiry learning activity, a thirty-second anecdote or illustration, or even just a memory tool. Stories are also a way to build trust and community in the classroom. When we share our stories, students trust us enough to share their own.

WHY USE STORIES?

I enjoy talking about abstract ideas. I like concepts like the "state of nature" scenario introduced at the beginning of Chapter 2—I don't always need context, characters, or a plotline to be engaged. But for most teenagers (and most adults), abstract concepts are difficult to grasp. They seem irrelevant and unimportant compared with the pressing concerns of daily life, like *What should I wear to school?* and *What will be on the test?* Abstract reasoning develops during adolescence, but we know that the prefrontal cortex is far from mature when students start high school at age fourteen.

When we introduce complex ideas like osmosis, consumer surplus, sound waves, or limits on the First Amendment, many high school students find it challenging to process the information—or even pay attention. We can use stories to disguise difficult concepts, to dress them up and make them understandable and interesting.

For fifteen years, I taught Civil Liberties, a junior-senior elective course focused on building students' understanding of personal rights and the US judicial system. I learned by trial and error that my students were able (or willing) to wrap their heads around complex legal questions only when they involved human interest stories. The more details, the better.

We spent a lot of time on the First Amendment, since it includes six rights, and I wanted the students to think deeply about questions such as *Should there be limits on free speech?* Their first response was usually a knee-jerk "no"—because they had always been taught that the United States is good, our Constitution is good, and rights are good. They could not think about limits in an abstract way.

But when I showed them the video *For Which It Stands*, a *story* about flag burning, the students finally got past their superficial understanding and started discussing the question of limits as if it mattered. The video features Joey Johnson, a self-proclaimed revolutionary communist, explaining in his own words why he burned the American flag outside the 1984 Republican National Convention as a protest against American imperialism, flag-protection statutes, and Ronald Reagan's patriotic appeal (*For Which It Stand*s 1992). The viewer learns about Johnson's childhood experiences during the Vietnam War, his philosophy, and his reasons for burning the flag. The viewer also hears veterans expressing their heartbreak at the burning flag and demonstrators, captured in news footage, shouting slogans like "Red, white and blue, we spit on you. You stand for plunder; you will go under."

The video made Johnson's protest visceral and real; it's a compelling story. Some of my students were appalled and wanted to see Johnson thrown in prison—or exiled. "Why does he still live here?" "If you don't love it, leave it!" Others argued that punishing speech is a worse sacrilege than burning the flag. One year, two students baked and decorated a "flag cake" and served slices to their classmates to make the point that if you outlaw desecration, you'd also have to outlaw a lot of Fourth of July traditions.

Peter Cole, one of my students in 2011–12, says he still remembers being offended by Johnson's actions, but he wavered on whether flag burning should be against the law (personal interview, December 22, 2016). What impressed him most was that there was an actual person named Joey Johnson, that *Texas v. Johnson* wasn't just a precedent to learn but a real controversy involving a real person. "The plaintiff—there was a principle at hand, and they fought for it, and it went all the way up to the Supreme Court," Peter says. "What I learned about civil liberties not only was what my rights are and how those have developed but, really, what we know about how those came to be."

The resolution to that story—the landmark Supreme Court decision in *Texas v. Johnson*—took on great personal importance for students on both sides. If the bell rang before they knew the outcome, kids would linger around my desk after class, pleading with me to tell them what actually happened. *"Did he go to prison?" "It is illegal to burn the flag now, isn't it?" "Doesn't this fit what we learned about clear and present danger, if you're starting a fire?"*

When we read the decision together, even weaker readers were able to work their way through some challenging legal wording because they wanted answers. Without the story hook, few students would have been emotionally invested in the nuances of protected speech or Justice Brennan's famous statement: "If there is a bedrock principle underlying the First Amendment, it is that the Government may not prohibit the expression of an idea simply because society finds the idea itself offensive or disagreeable" (Chicago-Kent College of Law at Illinois Tech 1989). Thanks to the story, Brennan's words became part of the students' understanding of the First Amendment, and they developed new questions in response to the case, such as *Why is an action (burning) considered speech? Does flag burning endanger people if it sparks violence? Why punish flag burning if burning is an approved way to retire a flag? Is cross burning also protected speech?*

Johnson won his case, by the way, and flag-protection statutes in forty-eight states were overturned by that decision. (Donald Trump reinvigorated that debate, so stay tuned.)

While high school teachers may be reluctant to emphasize stories, thinking them more appropriate for elementary or middle school (or too time-consuming), politicians, lawyers, and businesspeople know the power of a good story to hook an audience. Ty Bennett, a motivational speaker who coaches business leaders on the art of sales, explains that compelling stories activate mirror neurons in the listeners, which helps them experience the story as if it happened to them. "If they experience it, then the *a-ha* moment, solution or conclusion to the story will become theirs. They will own it. They will absorb it and adopt it, and when they do, they become much more compliant and interested in you and in your objectives" (Bennett 2014, 45–49). Bennett says there are seven reasons stories engage listeners more effectively than straight facts:

1. Stories are common ground between speaker and audience.

2. Stories ignite the imagination and the senses.

3. Stories are a safe way to reveal our priorities and sense of self.

4. Stories are more memorable than facts.

5. Stories are retold.

6. Stories stimulate a response in the audience.

7. Stories reveal purpose and meaning. (47–49)

Although Bennett writes for a business audience, his reasons reveal why storytelling is effective for high school student engagement. When you share a story with students—or they share a story with you—you immediately form a common bond of experience. When I tell my psychology students how my

Dalmatian puppy suffered "learned helplessness" when she failed at leaping over a gate (and never tried again), and they tell me how the "overjustification effect" of parental encouragement (or worse yet, grades) ruined their love of playing guitar or reading, we start to know and understand each other better, revealing something about ourselves and creating common ground.

I started out telling stories early in my teaching career because it seemed like an easy way to hook students and explain complex ideas. They paid attention, rather than zoning out. But I didn't realize how powerful the students' emotional involvement would be. When you tell students stories like the ER mistake story or the Joey Johnson story, they imagine themselves as the doctor or Johnson or one of the veterans offended by flag burning. They retell the story to their friends at lunch and to their families at dinner, strengthening neural connections and making retrieval easier later—even much later.

Tao Wu, one of my students in 2010–11, says he still vividly remembers many of the free speech cases we talked about in Civil Liberties years ago, including the Johnson case, the claims of Holocaust deniers, and the arrest of 2 Live Crew for public obscenity in Florida (personal interview, November 9, 2016). He also remembers the deep questions these cases raised. "If you want freedom, what kinds of things qualify as freedom of speech? What happens if your freedom starts to affect others?" says Tao. "Facts are kind of dry. It's much easier for me to apply the concepts of one case to another."

Tao did not have a strong opinion about Johnson's case—he was new to the United States at the time and not strongly attached to the flag—but the story taught him a lot about American culture and democracy. "Even though the gesture would be deemed by most as unpatriotic and a poor reflection of the United States, it was nevertheless protected under the Bill of Rights," he says. "I was amazed that there was a system in place to help Johnson, a high school dropout communist who was extremely unpopular among the general public, to defend his individual rights against the most powerful nation in the world."

Bennett (2014) says stories reveal our purpose and meaning. In the classroom, that means we can use stories to give our students a reason to care. Delores Liston (1994), an education professor at Georgia Southern University, explains that when we distill course material into pertinent facts only—like lists of key terms to be memorized—we are actually making it more difficult for students to learn. She used the example of geography, which is frequently taught as maps filled with cities, rivers, and mountains. When students learn geography through relevant stories about people and communities, the stories connect with students' neural networks and personal experiences and create relevant, lasting knowledge.

One of the best ways to build this relevance is to tell students stories about other young people. That's why *The Diary of a Young Girl* by Anne Frank (1990) and *The Book Thief* by Markus Zusak (2007) resonate so strongly with teenage readers.

One of my goals was for Civil Liberties students to understand procedural details, like how court cases are argued, how precedent is used, and how opinions and dissents are written, which can be kind of dry. For their first taste of procedure, I used *Tinker v. Des Moines* (1969), a case about public school students who were suspended for wearing black armbands to protest the Vietnam War in the early '60s.

I started out, like Steve Rubino did with his class, by telling a detailed, personalized story about how the Tinkers, their parents, and other families met one chilly December night in Des Moines to strategize their protest against the Vietnam War, and how a student journalist (in attendance) actually tipped off district administrators that students would be wearing black armbands to school. I told them about John Tinker, who was fifteen, and how nervous he was, how he didn't even want to wear the armband and wore it over a black suit jacket, but drew attention when he changed clothes for gym class. I told them about Mary Beth Tinker, who was only in middle school and was teased by boys about her armband.

When the students role-played the arguments aloud and read the decision, they were absorbed in the story and their own responses. They could not believe that the Tinkers and their friend Christopher Eckhardt (who was attending the University of Minnesota and missed the Supreme Court oral arguments because he was stranded by a blizzard at the airport), were actually punished for something as innocuous as wearing plain black armbands.

"It made me think, if I'm passionate about this issue and use my rights in the school room, how would this look? Should I be allowed to do such a thing?" Peter Cole recalled.

The students didn't even realize they were absorbing a lesson on Supreme Court procedure—or that they were preparing their brains to learn and reason about similar cases.

Andrew Larkin was in my class when the "Bong Hits 4 Jesus" case (*Morse v. Frederick*) was argued before the Supreme Court (personal interview, December 19, 2016). Joseph Frederick, a high school student in Alaska, had tested students' free speech rights yet again by unfurling a banner saying "Bong Hits 4 Jesus" across the street from his school as the Olympic Torch Relay passed through town. My Civil Liberties class that year had already studied *Tinker*, so the new case added some suspense. Black armbands were protected, we knew that, but how far would the court go with speech? Would the school succeed in trying to punish Frederick? (As it turns out, yes.)

Andrew says this case really got his attention because he and his friends fashioned themselves "would-be protesters," and he thought the facts of the case were funny. "I remember not feeling that this world was accomplishing anything by clamping down on it. I could see it being one of my friends who got in trouble for it," Andrew says. "I wanted to know what happened."

As Newkirk (2014) points out repeatedly, stories are not just for English and social studies; they are essential to our understanding of every aspect of human knowledge. If we can teach law as a series of decisions, why not teach science as a process of wonder and discovery and experimentation? Edward O. Wilson, a world-renowned biologist and entomologist, explained in an essay on storytelling that he started every science class he taught at Harvard with the big picture: *What is life? What is the meaning of life?* "Once you've got the attention of the audience, then you break the big questions down into stories, little dramas, that expose the trial and error process of science and the ideas that animate and move it forward" (Wilson 2002, 11).

The most difficult discipline for storytelling might be math; so much of high school math is abstract and theoretical. But Scott Steketee, a University of Pennsylvania professor who taught for eighteen years in the Philadelphia Public Schools, is one of many educators trying to change that perception (personal interview, August 4, 2016). He believes that students also learn math better when they start with concrete, relevant examples and then move gradually to the abstract mathematical concept.

Teachers can use real-world situations, even comedic stories, to teach math concepts, he says. For example, Steketee says, an online Mathalicious lesson called "You're So Fined" uses a John Oliver broadcast explaining how traffic tickets and other civil fines can escalate to ridiculous sums (http://www.mathalicious.com/lessons/you-re-so-fined). Oliver, who hosts the HBO talkshow *Last Week Tonight with John Oliver*, is a clever storyteller; he uses outrage, harsh language, and choice details to hook listeners on his point. The lesson takes the Oliver story about compounding fees and turns it into an examination of linear equations. "Concepts of mathematics come into play in all kinds of areas in the real world," Steketee says.

Storytelling isn't just about getting students to learn content, though. It's also about building relationships. In my first few years of teaching, I wanted to connect with my students, but looking back I realize I never knew very much about them. One of my eighth-grade girls was obsessed with Kurt Cobain. One had a very cute baby sister. One boy was narcoleptic. That's about it. In class, we talked about Anne Frank. We talked about red herrings in Agatha Christie's *And Then There Were None*. We talked about commas and semicolons. We didn't talk enough about what the students wanted from life, what they were afraid of, whom they could trust.

When you share stories with students, that changes. Over the years, I've told students funny stories about my children's first words, my dogs' antics, my travel mishaps. I've told them about my frustrations trying out for high school sports (always cut) and trying to get my first newspaper internship (sixty-five rejection letters!). I've also told them about losing both of my parents to dementia, what that was like, and how it changed me.

In return, students have shared their funny experiences, daily frustrations, and stories about family vacations, sibling behavior, sports accomplishments, and favorite movies with me. Some have shared deeply personal stories, either with the entire class or with me personally. Some have told stories of their mistreatment due to race or sexual orientation. Others have talked about how violent crime affected their family or how they lost a parent to suicide or a drug overdose.

I remember one student who always presented himself as an arrogant know-it-all in class. When we talked about right-to-die cases, physician-assisted suicide, and care of terminally ill patients in Civil Liberties, he became uncharacteristically quiet. He surprised me by coming in after school, wanting to talk about this issue more. He couldn't stop thinking about what he would do if he were paralyzed or terminally ill, and he wanted to talk about how it would affect his parents. After that conversation, he toned down his attitude and started listening more to his classmates.

Teenagers want to be heard and acknowledged, even (or especially) the difficult ones. When we listen, we can change the way they engage in our classes.

Beth Bernstein-Yamashiro, writing in *New Directions for Youth Development*, explains that personal connections between students and teachers are not simply "special additions" for the students but "learning opportunities of their own" (2004, 56). Students feel anxious and lose motivation when their teachers are rigid and impersonal, when they don't try to make those connections. She quoted one student as saying that when a teacher doesn't try to connect, "You're so upset with the teacher, you can't even sit there and learn." But "any attempt by teachers to break the ice or express caring made an enormous difference to students' interest, confidence and motivation" (2004, 58). When we share stories and listen to students' stories, we open a new pathway for engaging and motivating our students.

HOW DO YOU INCLUDE STORIES IN YOUR INSTRUCTION?

I never set out to be a storyteller, and I really can't remember the first stories I ever told in class. Over time, as I saw students struggle to understand legal concepts, economic theories, and psychology terms, I started to turn examples and explanations into stories, probably as a result of my experience in journalism.

In classes like Civil Liberties, history, and psychology, there are plenty of stories available—we just have to scratch the surface a little. It would be hard to teach psychology without telling the story of Phineas Gage, whose accident with a tamping iron thrust a railroad spike through his face in 1848, causing his personality to change (despite his normal cognitive skills). Or Henry Moliason, H. M., whose hippocampus was removed in an effort to stop seizures, causing him to lose all ability to form new memories. I found an NPR story with an interview of H. M. (http://www.npr.org/templates/story/story.php?storyId=7584970), and we listen to it in class. Students grimace when they hear that poor man's voice saying, "I can't remember that either" over and over.

Like math, economics can also be a little more challenging; there aren't a lot of famous, compelling case studies. We can talk about the Depression or the recent recession, but it's harder to find cases that illustrate abstract concepts like elasticity, comparative advantage, and monopoly market structures. Instead, I've collected a lot of little examples from my own life. Found a jacket on sale? File that away for consumer surplus. Compared tomato prices at a farmers' market and found they were all the same? Use that to explain perfect competition.

When I was on vacation in Merida, Mexico, with my family about ten years ago, we stopped in a bodega to pick up some Trident gum for our flight home. My sons—not yet teenagers—had gotten used to translating prices from pesos into dollars, at an exchange rate of about eight pesos to the dollar.

The older one picked up a pack of gum and told me excitedly, "It's only four pesos!"

I said, "That's a pretty good deal."

He said, "At home, gum costs more than a dollar! More than twice as much!

"You know what we should do?" he proposed, wheels turning. "We should buy as much gum as we can find, and we could get a big truck and bring it all back to the United States, and we could sell it!"

"Uhh . . . no," I told him. "We're not doing that. We're not going into business reimporting Trident gum."

It's a simple story, and I embellish it a little by dramatizing our parts. My students always think it's funny, and it's a nice illustration of exchange rates, purchasing power parity, and even arbitrage. "That's a good idea," my students say. And they ask me, "Do you seriously think about economics all the time?"

Peter Bohacek (personal interview, June 1, 2016), the Minnesota physics teacher, was living in Berkeley when the Loma Prieta earthquake happened in 1989. His brother was living in Santa Cruz, and his house collapsed. Bohacek said he was on the phone with his sister-in-law, and she screamed, "There's an aftershock, there's an aftershock," and he was puzzled because he wasn't feeling it. "And then BAM, the aftershock hit me," he said. "I'm about seventy miles away, and it took about ten seconds between when she communicated to me about the aftershock and when I felt the aftershock. And I thought, 'That's all you need to measure the velocity of an earthquake wave propagating through the surface of the earth.'" He tells that story every year.

Mike Lampert, a physics teacher in Salem, Oregon, talks about his mom's baking when he explains how batteries work (personal interview, June 16, 2016). "I tell them, 'You know, I never eat my mom's cookies.' When you start out a story like that, they go, *You don't eat your mom's cookies?* I explain that she would take the dough, line the cookie pan with foil, then put it in the oven. As it cooked, the foil would get into the crevasses of the cookie dough. When I would bite into it, the foil would react with my fillings, which are a different metal, and I have acid in my mouth, which forms a battery," Lampert says. "It sticks in their mind."

Lampert also tells deeply serious stories, like when he's explaining the force of airbags. He wants his students to understand the dangers of driving without seat belts, drinking and driving, texting and driving. He has his students simulate a car crash using software, and he has them develop a threshold of force that is safe. The law requires that an individual be able to survive a head-on collision at 30 mph with passive restraints, he tells them, and he shows them what that looks like by blowing up an old airbag in class.

Then he tells them about a student, Samantha, who took a hairpin turn too quickly and died in a car crash. She was a brilliant young scientist, just a month away from presenting research in Boston. She was out to dinner before prom with friends and took a shortcut on a dangerous road; she died wearing her prom dress.

Casey Chaffin, one of Lampert's students, said she learned more than just physics from him (personal interview, December 20, 2016). She learned from his stories how deeply he cares about his students—not just Samantha but all of them. "He wants kids to think about the world and how they impact it, and how it impacts them."

What can we do if we don't have a story to illustrate a particular lesson? We haven't all exchanged currencies or felt earthquakes, and we don't all have tragic stories, or at least not ones we want to share. Fictional stories, like the narrative about Tom, the new ER resident, can work well too.

Jen Nippert and Eric Friberg, the Henry Sibley High School biology teachers, realized their students were bored by protein synthesis, a very dry concept for fifteen-year-olds. They decided to create a fictional story about a baby who gets sick. When her mother takes her to the doctor, the doctor draws blood samples. They show students the fictional test results, comparing a normal red blood cell to the baby's red blood cell, which has sickle cell anemia, and talk about why the difference is important. "It's a drawn-out saga," Nippert says. Both teachers keep a picture of the fictional baby on their wall all year to pique interest.

If you're creating a fictional case study, you have a lot more control over the story line. According to the National Center for Case Study Teaching in Science (Herreid 2005), these tips help create a thought-provoking case:

> Keep the story short.
>
> Include conflict and a dilemma that is both open-ended and relevant to the students.
>
> Create interesting characters and dialogue.
>
> Make it a contemporary issue (and a real one) if possible.
>
> Address specific learning objectives.

It's also important to give the story life—and not just make it a convenient example. If I told my students, "I was in Mexico, and with the eight-pesos-to-one-dollar exchange rate, gum was actually cheaper," that would not make for a memorable story. It takes the dramatization, the impersonation of an entrepreneurial kid, to make the story stick.

Filmmakers also have good advice about how to create effective stories. Jason McDonald, a professor of instructional psychology and technology at Brigham Young University, interviewed eight successful filmmakers to find out what principles they use to engage and educate audiences—and how those can be used to create better instructional environments. The filmmakers stressed the importance of knowing your audience and including conflict, authenticity, and entertainment. Also, they said, you should leave some details unstated, so listeners have a challenge.

McDonald quoted one producer, saying, "It's a much more rewarding experience as a film viewer if I put something together that I think nobody else got'" (McDonald 2009, 116).

If this sounds complicated, it doesn't need to be. The point is really to put a human face on whatever we are teaching, to make the lesson about people and conflicts and choices rather than dry facts.

We can also encourage students to share their stories instead of always being the storytellers ourselves. Students may not have expertly crafted stories, but they have experiences they can share to help illustrate what they are learning, and many times their experiences are more relevant than ours.

In Robin Moten's English class in suburban Detroit, students of different races and ethnicities talked about their responses to violence and police shootings, and many shared deeply personal stories (classroom observation, September 23, 2016). One student explained how she felt after the June 2016 Orlando nightclub shooting—how she could not sit still in classes and had to excuse herself to sit in the bathroom and calm down. Another told how he was bullied for stuttering in elementary school. Moten talked with her students about the challenges she faces as an African American teacher in a predominantly white school, trying to figure out her responsibility to promote safe spaces for discussion about these issues. "When I became a teacher, that was always the goal: as-honest-as-possible dialogue and treating kids not as stupid 'just kids' or as 'mini-mes' but as folks who were developing, and some of whom were going to be very different from me," Moten says.

My students have also shared many stories through the years, ranging from light anecdotes to deeply serious, personal experiences. In a few different classes, I have asked students to tell their stories through writing assignments, including a "Defining Moment" essay assigned in Journalism 2 and a "Who am I?" personality paper assigned in AP Psychology.

I got the idea for the "Defining Moment" assignment at a journalism conference several years ago, and it seemed like a good way to help students get beyond the obvious—*What is your favorite movie? What is your favorite color?*—when writing practice feature stories about each other. One junior girl wrote in great detail about struggling to learn to read in first grade and how it made her feel to watch everyone else move to chapter books while she was still working on picture books. One sophomore girl, Maddy Rosenow, wrote about how a particularly rigid coach destroyed her love of basketball. A sophomore boy, Ryan Yoch, wrote about his experiences being bullied and left out of the social scene at the private school he once attended. I never would have guessed. (See Chapter 3, Samples 1 and 2 in the appendix.)

Stories like these help students learn to write better journalistic features; they also helped form a strong, close-knit community within the newspaper staff. Ryan observed, "It built a trust and a friendship that made everything easier once we eventually became editors on the paper together" (personal interview, November 24, 2016).

WHAT ARE THE CHALLENGES OF USING STORYTELLING?

Storytelling is a great way for us to engage and motivate students—both because it helps store information efficiently in long-term memory and because it creates strong student-teacher relationships. It makes our classes less boring. Building stories into the curriculum can be challenging, though, if you have never done it. Here are tips to address a few of the challenges:

1. **Finding effective, compelling stories for every concept is not easy.** This is especially difficult for new teachers. "You're alive fifty years and you accumulate stories like that," Bohacek says. It is not always possible to borrow other teachers' stories, either. When I explain the difference between cross-sectional and longitudinal studies in AP Psych, I can talk about my own participation in Michael Reese Hospital's longitudinal study on adolescence when I was a kid, but that story really works only for me. It's important to build up your own stories over time, either in your own memory bank or by keeping a journal of events that spark an idea.

2. **Telling stories about yourself requires balance.** Remember that it's not all about you. Telling your own stories—as opposed to published cases or fictional stories—works best when the stories are authentic and humble (and funny). Sharing stories that paint you as a hero or a genius does not help build connections with students. They are already insecure enough about the perfect lives their friends seem to be living on social media. Students need reassurance that the adults in their lives have difficult or sad stories as well as happy ones, that real people have warts and can show resilience. Brief, self-deprecating stories with a

sense of humor work best. One student I interviewed, a high school freshman in Los Angeles, told me she cannot stand teachers who talk about themselves for no reason. If your stories are self-indulgent, overly personal, or attention-seeking, do not tell them.

3. **Telling stories effectively takes practice.** Filmmakers, authors, journalists, and actors work hard at learning to tell stories. They think about how to introduce the conflict, how to write realistic dialogue, how to build tension, and how much to reveal in the resolution. You need to know your audience and know what they are interested in, and you need to use stories that connect the content to the students in a meaningful way. You must appeal to multiple senses, so use images, vocalization, body language, and facial expressions. A large part of storytelling is the performance. If a story falls flat, think about how to retool it, or just discard it and start over.

4. **Storytelling must be part of a larger plan.** Taking a brief pause from a PowerPoint to tell a quick story, then returning to the dry list of facts is not enough. Use a story to encourage students to share their stories, or use a story as the basis for a discussion (Chapter 4) or Problem-Based Learning assignment (Chapter 5). After I tell the story about my son's gum-buying idea in Mexico, I encourage students to share their experiences with exchanging currency—some as immigrants to this country and some as travelers in other countries. Telling their own stories makes the learning much more powerful than just listening to mine.

TIPS FOR TEACHERS

How do I get started if I'm not a storyteller?
Start small. Pick one or two learning objectives that you could illustrate with a personal story or case study, then develop an effective story with a conflict and narrative structure. Practice telling it before using it in class.

Encourage student storytelling by using icebreakers in class, such as "two truths and a lie," where each student reveals three surprising facts about themselves, one of which isn't true–and their classmates have to guess which one is a lie. That encourages some creative storytelling and performance.

How can I build on my use of stories, if I'm already doing this?
Identify concepts students struggle with, like protein synthesis, and develop high-interest stories that you can use to increase attention and memory.

Encourage students to pair-share their own stories applying a difficult concept.

Use thought-provoking classroom questions (for example, *Is your "personality" the same at home and at school?*) or written assignments to create a safe, supportive environment for students to share their stories.

How will I assess and know if it's effective?

Use the same assessments you are using now to compare the effectiveness of teaching with stories. I use stories to help my psychology and economics students understand and remember terms and theories—especially difficult ones—and I can see their improvement on our unit exams.

Use anonymous student-connectedness surveys to evaluate how students perceive the classroom environment and their relationship with you.

4

DISCUSSION AND DEBATE: TRUST STUDENTS TO DRIVE MEANINGFUL CONVERSATION

As students take their seats around a large square table, Robin Moten wrestles with how to frame her question.

These students—a mix of freshmen, sophomores, juniors, and seniors—have read Nickel and Dimed: On (Not) Getting By in America by Barbara Ehren-reich. They have watched Robert Reich's Inequality for All. Now they've listened to Michael Seneski, the director of corporate strategy for Ford Motor Company, explain Ford's global strategies to them—in person.

Moten wants students to start connecting the dots. She won't tell them what to think—she won't even define the topic, globalization, for them. After several false starts, she finally settles on the question: "How have the *stories we've encountered so far, even though they are rooted in quantitative language, helped—no, encouraged—us to step outside of ourselves?"*

After a few minutes of writing, the students ease into their discussion, eventually wending their way to talking about the human cost of efficiency.

"People are losing jobs to robots. . . . We are basically going to be run by things that can do it themselves. I personally am scared of the autonomous car. What if it fails? What if it has a power outage?" one student says.

"I'm going to counter that. Something like 90 percent of accidents are human error."

Moten interjects to steer the conversation: "Is this the story we're interested in building, about efficiency and reducing human error?"

"That's what I found the most disturbing part. . . . The whole human part was really disregarded. We're really disregarding unskilled labor. If we don't fix the education system, we're leaving a whole lot of people without jobs in the name of efficiency. It's hard to see how we're moving toward losing opportunities for those people."

"Are we just coming to a world that's about efficiency? They're taking away our humanity."

"Why do we value humanity?"

The students' conversation veers again into auto safety, speeding tickets, and police officers, then circles back to the larger issue: efficiency versus humanity.

"Can I just butt in right now?" says a student who has been standing off to the side. "In Robert Reich's video, when people in the middle class are losing their jobs due to these automatic cars, that's not better for the economy."

"You have a good point, but the question is whether the productivity is there."

"Why would we want to make something that will lose jobs for other people?"

"But you are raising the standard of living."

"When did this obsession with efficiency come about?"

When the period ends, the students are still wrestling with these complex issues. What is a company's obligation to its community or nation? What is a consumer's responsibility? Where will the pressure for efficiency lead us? What options will low-skilled workers have? Could we stop globalization or automation if we wanted to? (classroom observation, September 23, 2016).

Reflecting on it later, one of the participants, Shannon Stall, said this kind of open discussion is the best way for her to learn (personal interview, September 23, 2016).

"People challenging what you think exposes you to more," Shannon says. "I definitely got a lot out of this discussion. I got to see business and morality in a different way than I just think of it."

WHAT ARE DISCUSSION AND DEBATE?

Step inside a traditional classroom. The teacher is talking and students are quiet, seated at their desks, watching. Are they listening? Are they learning? We think so because we are so accustomed to this model. But we don't know what is going on in the students' minds. We have no idea if they are tuned in or thinking about last night's argument with a friend.

In a discussion-based class or classroom debate, students are the ones talking. They are asking the questions, disagreeing with each other, helping each other, clarifying their own understanding, and sometimes saying things that are completely wrong—putting their misunderstandings out in the open, where they can be addressed. This teaching strategy takes many forms, including open-ended, whole-class discussion (the predominant model in Moten's combined English and social studies classroom), small-group discussion, or more formal debate or deliberation.

But not every form of student talk is "discussion" or "debate." In fact, much of what we call discussion in our high school classrooms is better described as traditional recitation or Initiation-Response-Evaluation. The teacher asks a question looking for a specific answer and either "cold-calls"—randomly choosing a student to respond—or looks for volunteers. Then the teacher briefly evaluates the response—right or wrong, possibly a shade of gray—before moving on to another question and another student response.

For example, look at the following exchange in my psychology class:

> *Me: When Bill can't remember his new girlfriend's phone number because he thinks of his old girlfriend's phone number instead, that's called what? Kevin, what kind of interference is it?*
>
> *Kevin: Retroactive interference?*

Me: Retroactive interference would be if he remembered the new number but couldn't remember the old one.

Kevin: Oh, then proactive.

Me: Yes, exactly.

This kind of "check for understanding" improves student engagement and retention compared with undiluted lecture, but it is not discussion. Genuine discussion or debate is a conversation among students, not a one-sentence attempt to provide the "right" answer.

In their 2003 study of sixty-four high school English classrooms, Judith Langer and Martin Nystrand found that only 1.7 minutes out of every 60 minutes of class time observed were spent in actual discussion, where students talked to each other, not the teacher, and knowledge developed through conversation. (They called it discussion if three students participated for at least thirty seconds—a pretty low bar.) Most of what Langer and Nystrand found instead was Initiation-Response-Evaluation combined with lecture and seat work. "Such instruction places a premium on transmission of information, providing very little room for the exploration of ideas, which is necessary for the development of deeper understanding" (Applebee et al. 2003, 689).

In Langer's earlier study on schools that "beat the odds," where students outperformed peers at schools with similar demographics, she observed that the most effective teachers used genuine discussion-based approaches to learning.

The features of discussions in these classrooms were

- "more use of authentic questions, which were used to explore different understandings rather than to 'test' what students might already know;

- "more time for open discussion: whole-class discourse devoted to free exchange of ideas among students or between at least three participants; and

- "more 'uptake,' in which a teacher's question 'took up' and built on a student's previous comment, creating continuity in the discourse" (Applebee et al. 2003, 690).

Let's revise my earlier dialogue with Kevin—about Bill and the girl-friend's phone number—to incorporate these criteria. Instead of just seeking a definition–term match, I might ask, "How have you experienced proactive or retroactive interference?" This question gives students the opportunity to practice and apply their understanding, as well as share stories. It also allows for multiple answers, so several students can respond, rather than just one. If a student answers incorrectly—for example, "When I couldn't remember my new locker combination because I kept thinking of the old one, that was retroactive interference"—I can facilitate more responses by saying, "Now, is that retroactive, if old knowledge interferes with new?" and offering the question to the class.

The focus is less on right or wrong answers, and more on exploring student understanding of (and experience with) the concepts.

There are many effective ways to structure (or unstructure) a genuine student discussion—giving students time to talk while they are solving problems in class, preparing a formal debate, asking students to share ideas in an online forum, or staging a congressional hearing. The key is to ask thoughtful questions and create expansive opportunities for students to exchange ideas and build their own understanding.

It doesn't always work right away. At the beginning of the free speech unit in Civil Liberties class, I would hand out a short news article about a neo-Nazi news conference in St. Paul. After students read it, I'd ask, "What do you think? Do neo-Nazis deserve free speech?" It seemed like a thought-provoking question (and topic), but it didn't work. The question was too broad, too ill-defined, and too risky; almost no one volunteered to answer.

It took a few changes to make that an effective conversation starter. In the revised lesson, I gave students the same article along with some "food for thought" questions to answer in their journals, like *Why did the group come to St. Paul? Why did they claim their speech was limited? Protesters (calling themselves Refuse and Resist) say they oppose all forms of repression—are they repressing the neo-Nazis? Do you have a free speech right to drown out someone else?* After the students had time to journal and gather their thoughts, I asked them, "If a hate group was coming to your community to say negative things about people like you, what do you think would be the best response?" The discussion was transformed. The new questions gave them time to think and made the issue more personal.

I think it's best to ignore them.

I don't think you can ignore them—they'll just grow bigger.

> *But if you show up and give them attention, that's what*
> *they want.*

I encouraged students to wait before critiquing each other's ideas. We put a list of possible responses on the board:

> *Ignore them.*
>
> *Have a counterprotest.*
>
> *Try to educate people.*
>
> *Pray for them.*
>
> *Tell them they can't come.*
>
> *Beat them up.*
>
> *Start a riot.*

Then they had time to discuss and debate each of the ideas, weigh the pros and cons. They referenced the news article I had given them: "What about the one guy who shows up to see what's going on? If you don't respond, he might think it's OK to join them." They also listened to each other and asked difficult questions, such as "If we silence them, don't we have to silence other groups?" The proposal to keep them out ("Tell them they can't come") brought us back to the point I wanted them to discuss: *Does everyone deserve free speech? And at what cost?* At the end of the hour, I told them the story of the 1977 court case *Nationalist Socialist Party of America v. Village of Skokie,* about the neo-Nazis' planned march in Skokie, Illinois. They were able to understand the court's reasoning—protecting the march as free speech— because they had already worked through the arguments themselves.

My role in this lesson wasn't to lecture my students on the law, or tell them what to think about hate speech, but to let them build understanding by providing a safe place for a difficult conversation. Not every discussion is as sensitive as this one, but discussion always requires the teacher to play a different role than in a traditional classroom. There's more listening than talking, more covert than overt instruction, and more focus on a climate of openness and respect than on silence and compliance.

WHY USE DISCUSSION?

The AP Psychology course outline has more than one hundred separate learning objectives, and most of them are compound; for example:

- Compare and contrast the major theories and approaches to explaining personality (e.g., psychoanalytic, humanist, cognitive, trait, social cognition, behavioral).

- Identify key contributors to personality theory (e.g., Alfred Adler, Albert Bandura, Paul Costa and Robert McCrae, Sigmund Freud, Carl Jung, Abraham Maslow, Carl Rogers).

Count them all individually, and it's more like seven hundred learning objectives. It's overwhelming. I could easily spend every class period plowing through PowerPoint slides and providing students with summary notes on every theory and theorist. That's basically how I was taught both world history and AP US History, and it was terribly boring. Students are far more engaged when they are able to talk about people and ideas as if they mean something.

For example, listen in as my AP Psych students discuss whether personality is fixed or changing, and whether psychological theory helps us understand personality (classroom observation, January 11, 2017).

> **Gillian Lerdahl:** *Who you are is super inherent. The things that happen around you can influence you to behave differently, but I don't think the deepest part of you changes.*

> **Kalei Cartwright:** *On that, what about the article that says people's personalities get better over time? How is that different from maturing, if people's personalities get better as they age?*

> **Lydia Grimes:** *That kind of calls into question, when is a trait a trait? When are our habits going to turn into "You have that trait now"? If it's just maturing, you would have to be born with the trait.*

> **Cameron Tomczyk:** *You know how people discredit Freud because they say, "If you can't study what's going on, it's not useful, so you shouldn't worry about the unconscious mind"? Isn't personality kind of the same way? You can say, "I guess it's obvious people are extroverted or introverted," but if you can't put it into a really*

specific operational definition that's not situationally based, then it's not really worth looking into.

Jonah Westerman: *I agree with Cameron. I think conversations about personality are inherently so hard to wrap your head around because you can't . . . There's no way to define the main points you make about personality. There's an inherent part of the human psyche you can't put into words or understand.*

These students are driving the discussion themselves, weaving together theory and personal experience, and trying to make sense of trait theory, the Myers-Briggs test, the person-situation controversy, and Freud's model of the mind.

It wasn't easy to make time for this discussion. My AP Psych class is blended—part in person, part online—so it meets face-to-face only twice a week. We have just three days together for the entire Personality unit. Day 1, I introduce Freudian theory, and the students perform mini-skits on defense mechanisms. (The rest of the theory notes are "flipped"—they are recorded and available on YouTube.) Day 2, I introduce the person-situation controversy, and students share stories about their own behavior in different settings. For Day 3, they read two short news articles about current research and prepare to answer these questions: *Which personality theory best explains who we are and how we act? Is personality stable? If not, then how do we define ourselves?*

In their discussion, which was run as an open-ended seminar, students deeply critiqued trait theory, dismissing any one test's ability to label or explain personality (and comparing the Myers Briggs Type Indicator—MBTI—to a horoscope). They were less certain about the stability of personality across situation and time. They kept coming back to this: *Is your personality only what you reveal, or is it the whole iceberg of your unconscious?*

Later in the discussion, Ben Ebert explained why his personality might vary in different situations: "When I meet someone for the first time, I'm not going to dive into the pool," he said. "You have stories you want to tell that further define yourself. You don't just like, on a first date, go into, 'here's how I was raised.'"

Emma Tsai pointed out that this doesn't necessarily mean his personality changes. "Even if you don't know fully somebody's personality all at once, you might only be getting layers of it, might it still not be all of the person's personality?"

We are so used to narrowly defining learning as the accumulation of specific facts—determined by political authorities, test writers, textbook publishers, and administrators—that we often ignore or downplay the kind of learning that takes place when students talk to each other like this. It seems unimaginable—preposterous, even—that open-ended student discussion could somehow lead to deeper understanding of important concepts. What if they don't do the reading? What if they don't prepare? It seems safer just to tell them the information, especially when time is short.

But students do learn from listening to each other and the theories (and theorists) become meaningful, rather than just more terms and names to memorize. Indiana University's High School Survey of Student Engagement—the same survey that found that 66 percent of high school students were bored in class every day—asked students what kinds of instruction they did find engaging. The number one answer, picked by 61 percent of students surveyed, was "discussion and debate" (Macklem 2015).

A group of professors at Hope College in Holland, Michigan, conducted focus groups with eighteen-to-twenty-one-year-old students to find out how to better engage them in discussion. The students said that when they're given a genuine opportunity to hash out their ideas, without fear that the instructor will punish them for "wrong" answers, discussion "helps them focus better, makes it easier to pay attention, and stops them from zoning out" (Roehling et al. 2011, 2).

It's clear students in discussion-oriented classrooms are more engaged. They are also more willing to test out ideas and opinions, more willing to help each other, more likely to build a deep understanding of their learning, and more empowered to advocate for their views in the world outside of school. It's worth the time.

TESTING IDEAS THROUGH DEBATE

Steve Jents, a social studies teacher at St. Paul Central High School, used a mini-debate format to help his economics students understand and think about President-Elect Trump's tax cut ideas—a very dry, complicated topic (classroom observation, December 15, 2016). Jents divided the class into two groups. Students facing the south wall of the classroom (Team B) read an editorial supporting Trump, while students facing north (Team A) read a critical article.

When they were done reading, the students stood with their respective teams and presented brief arguments. A student for Team B started, "Our author talked about how a large tax cut would be beneficial to the economy and cause more growth and more jobs, like Reagan's big tax cut did. And how they should divide it into two brackets . . ."

His teammate added, "Our group was in favor of the article. As people get tax cuts, they have more money to spend. With making it smaller, less tax brackets, we're actually saving money on collecting taxes."

A student on Team A replied, "But in the Reagan era, taxes for the highest income earners were at 70 percent. That's very different from our present situation. Back then they helped soften the blow of inflation. That's not what they would do now. When you look at Bush's administration, he did a bunch of large tax cuts, and all of them hurt the economy."

A Team B student responded and critiqued Team A's source. "He's [the article's author] not really an authority on what Trump is going to do. He used to be part of the Republican Party but hates what it has become. He's untrustworthy, not unbiased."

The mini-debate continued for about five to seven minutes, with students adding pieces of evidence and insights. When it wrapped up, Jents praised their comments and encouraged the students to always question sources. "You don't have to listen to that. You don't have to listen to me," he said. "It's really important to have a well-rounded view of everybody's take on this."

The articles Jents provided, published by Reuters and *Forbes* magazine, were both from legitimate news sources, but he stressed the importance of always researching the authors as well as reading their viewpoints—a critical point in today's climate. "What do we know about Steve Forbes?" he asked them at the end. "What do we know about Bartlett [the author of the Reuters article]?" The students were quick to point out their backgrounds and biases—that Forbes himself ran for president twice, and that Bruce Bartlett helped institute Reagan's tax cuts.

The students learned a lot even from this brief conversation. First, they read the articles with a purpose and quickly processed important information: Trump's proposal, Reagan's tax cuts, Bush's tax cuts, and the contrasting economic periods. They also listened closely to each other, since they had to respond impromptu to information from the opposing side. They researched the sources (albeit briefly) and thought critically about their biases. Finally, they tested out ideas. They probably weren't sure after a brief debate whether they agreed with Trump's tax proposal, but they had started to think about it, and at the end, Jents let the students switch sides, so they had a few minutes to formulate and voice their own opinions.

"In theory, what Forbes says about economics sounds very good," one student said. "We just cut out the government, cut out the middle-man. We spend it however we want."

Another responded, "Does it make more sense to have the government handle money because they just spend money; they don't save money?"

Jents then tied it back to the circular flow diagram, reviewing how savings is a leakage from the economy and helping students understand that there is no easy answer to this issue.

LEARNING FROM EACH OTHER

In discussions and debates, students often help each other figure out difficult concepts. In the following excerpts from one of my AP Microeconomics students' online forums, students are helping each other decide whether Google is a monopoly and whether it should be treated as a public utility and therefore regulated.

The students post initial answers and then respond to each other. I follow along but only rarely interject comments.

> *I believe Google should be considered a monopoly because of the control they have over search engines, email, YouTube, Chrome, etc. In addition, the fact that they own over 24 major data centers scattered around the world that are used for storage, search and analytics addresses the fact that Google has much control over consumers, even if they do not realize it. . . . But I don't believe that Google could be seen as a public utility . . . typically a public utility is more similar to a consumer's necessity, but Google is completely for the consumer's benefit and is not a necessity.*

> *I think the reasons that you gave for why Google isn't a public utility are very interesting. But we also technically don't need electricity to survive either, right? I feel like a public utility means that the good*

*is necessary to consumers' lifestyles, like Google is
because so many people use the Internet.*

*I like your reason for why Google is a monopoly, but
I also think Google is now needed almost as much
as electricity because of how much people depend
on it.*

*Your point on how Google is very diversified is
interesting, and how that relates to whether or not it
is a public good. Is Google still nonexcludable and
nonrivalrous? I think it would fit these definitions.*

*I agree with your point 1, but for point 2, not all
public goods necessarily have to be a necessity.*

In this conversation, several students are wrestling with the meaning of
public utility and *public good* as well as *monopoly*, and they're not quite sure
about the definitions. Are public utilities always necessities? Are they always
public goods? They are figuring it out, and they raised interesting questions
and surfaced some misunderstandings. (Neither Google nor electricity fits
the strict definition of a public good, which I explained to the students later
in a class seminar. Utilities are generally necessities, but whether the Internet
is a necessity today is certainly a gray area.)

Anne Marciano's precalculus class at Arthur Johnson High School in
New Jersey has similar conversations, where students bounce ideas off each
other as they build their understanding of mathematical concepts (classroom
observation, October 14, 2016). At the beginning of their unit on sine, cosine,
and tangent, the students worked in small groups to graph data from angles,
then described what they saw. "Guys, I don't know how to do the fraction
part," one student said, and another leaned in to help. "Is inverse negative?"
one asked. Another replied, "Inverse is one over."

When they got to describing the sine waves, Marciano encouraged them
to be detailed and creative. There isn't just one answer.

"Can we say it's squiggly? It's repeating?" one student asked.

"What do you think of this description—I said it looks like a roller coaster."

Marciano added, "An observation can be that they have numbers."

"They're parabolic," a student added.

"It looks like ribbons in the wind when you do this," another said, making a wave motion.

"Waves, there you go. Waves," Marciano added.

By the end of the hour, with Marciano's subtle guidance, the students had shifted their vocabulary to more technical terms, like *periodic*, *symmetrical*, and *sinusoid axis*. She wants them to get there as much as possible on their own.

DEEP LEARNING

Another critical benefit of discussion is that students learn to think for themselves and develop a deeper, more enduring understanding of the material than do students who learn by passive listening. Mary Chin attended Phillips Exeter Academy, which innovated the use of discussion-based methods (called the Harkness Method) in math class. She found when she went to MIT as an undergraduate that her understanding of math was deeper than her peers' understanding (personal interview, September 30, 2016). "My peers knew these formulas way better than I did, memorized, but it would get to something that would be a little off, and it was clear they didn't have the same foundational understanding I did of the calculus," Chin says. "They would say, 'derivative,' but they were not as quick to recognize it as slope. To me, that was so much more important, that I could understand what was happening."

Chin now also uses this method to teach math at Arete Preparatory Academy in Arizona. Students listen and learn better from each other, she says. "I could say something to the class and say, 'OK, talk about it,' and I overhear another student say *verbatim* what I just said to the student next to them, and the student is, like, 'Oh!' . . . It's just something about teenagers—sometimes that other boy needs to hear it from a fifteen-year-old boy," she says.

In Civil Liberties class, discussion and debate helped students dive deeper and see the complexity of the issues we discussed, many of which initially seem like open-and-shut cases to teenagers. Alex Wald, a former student, says there were many times in class when he thought he knew the "right" answer to an issue, but then found himself changing his mind through discussion (personal interview, December 27, 2016). "Having been both deeply right and deeply wrong helped me realize there's a lot to be gained from discussion, and from asking probing questions rather than hearing somebody's opinion and immediately needing to decide if it's right or wrong," Alex says.

Alex and Peter Cole (personal interview, December 22, 2016) were on opposing sides of the "right to die" debate in their class, and they have continued that conversation for years, unable to reach any kind of satisfactory resolution. The more you know, the more difficult it is to decide, they say.

"You're balancing the right of a person to die versus the slippery slope of devaluing life to a degree," Peter says. "And you get into issues of capacity. It's difficult not to measure that on a case-by-case basis. Belgium has really liberal laws, and even people with severe depression can end their lives. Those cases have been broached, and also with minors, or people who maybe have a kid with a disability. There's just a bunch of different caveats to it."

Alex feels much the same. "Honestly, to this day I'm not super firm in my belief. It's such a nuanced issue," he says. "There were complex examples [in class], like the case of Terri Schiavo, where her husband—she was a vegetable, and her husband decided to pull the plug and marry somebody else. But we watched that video of the guy who lived on the ranch with his wife and couldn't even go to the bathroom by himself. He didn't want to go through the agony [of dying from ALS]. How could you deny him that right, when he's making the decision for himself?"

EMPOWERING

The opportunity to discuss issues in this manner is also empowering for students. When Tao Wu took Civil Liberties, he had lived in the United States for three years and still had limited English skills (personal interview, November 9, 2016). He had attended a top-ranked school in China, but instruction there was highly targeted to standardized tests. Although his math skills were strong, he had only superficial knowledge of world events and even less knowledge of the US political and judicial systems.

The opportunity to debate issues like physician-assisted suicide, gun control, and school prayer was completely new to him, and it motivated him to learn the necessary vocabulary, concepts, and facts. Tao says he realized he could not make a solid argument if he didn't know what the Constitution said, what the Supreme Court had ruled, or what research on these issues showed.

"Debate helps you think more critically and shape your entire thinking process," he says. "What evidence do I already know? What concepts do I already know to help me argue? Through arguing, I got feedback from other students that my thinking is flawed. If my thinking is flawed, what can I change? How can I fill that hole? For me, it gave me the motivation to learn certain facts so I could argue with people."

Tao says the experience also helped him develop more English fluency, since he was constantly working on verbal skills in class. "I was only able to speak conversational English; I wasn't able to present a belief in English efficiently or convey an argument," he says. "The course pretty much gave me both opportunities and motivation to elevate my English proficiency and learn how to persuade someone else."

Classroom discussion and debate also help students develop essential civic and workplace skills that they may not learn otherwise. Students do not instinctively know how to engage in a deep conversation—that skill must be taught and practiced. Some children and teenagers have never experienced thoughtful discussion or argumentation in their homes, and some are discouraged from learning this skill by gender or cultural norms.

Michael Firmin, Aaron Vaughn, and Amanda Dye (2007), researchers who studied the effectiveness of debate as a teaching strategy, said teaching girls and women to assert themselves in classroom discussion and debate is key to promoting gender equality. Learning to discuss and debate is also empowering for low-income and minority students. If disadvantaged students don't have these opportunities to learn civic skills, they won't learn how to thoughtfully discuss difficult issues, like Peter and Alex did. They won't learn the vocabulary of persuasion, like Tao did. They won't develop the belief that their voices count, that what they think matters to society, and they will continue to be sidelined in the political process.

Voter turnout among poor and minority groups is already much lower than turnout for middle-class whites. The students with a more privileged education will continue to accrue privileges, compounding the achievement gap. We need to teach the skills of discussion and debate to everyone to level the playing field.

HOW DO YOU INCLUDE DISCUSSION AND DEBATE IN YOUR INSTRUCTION?

In my first few years of teaching, my "discussions" looked mostly like the recitations Langer and Nystrand describe (Applebee et al. 2003). I asked questions and tried to get students to talk to each other, but with little success. When they responded, they usually made eye contact with me, seeking my stamp of approval. They were not discussing; they were performing—and I had to restate their responses and ask follow-up questions to get them to even listen to each other.

My assignment in 1998 to teach Civil Liberties—an elective course with no state-mandated content, no district-approved assessment, and no textbook or syllabus—was a turning point. My first semester teaching Civil Liberties was mostly a disaster. I thought students would be eager to engage with topics like free speech, gun control, and privacy rights, and I could just lob questions at them and wait for the fun to begin.

Instead, most of the students—all second-semester seniors, many of them already deep into "senior slide"—engaged halfheartedly and complained about being placed in my section rather than with another teacher, who was known for showing a lot of interesting (and controversial) videos. I struggled to get them to discuss or write in any meaningful way.

I'll never forget the flag-burning debate that shut down when one student said, "Respect the flag. Period" and threw up his hands. That was his team's entire argument, and no one wanted to challenge him. The two students on the opposing side had made a legitimate argument using the precedent of *Texas v. Johnson*, analogies to other protected speech (like hate speech), and emotional quotes about the power of the First Amendment. They were prepared, while his team had nothing but his statement. The class sat watching in stunned silence, and I asked if anyone wanted to add to the argument. No one did. I awkwardly asked the debaters to return to their seats, and we ended on an uncomfortable note.

The following summer, I dedicated myself to developing clear goals and a coherent outline for the course. I divided the curriculum into four units: Freedom of Speech/Second Amendment, Freedom of Religion, Right to Privacy, and Criminal Justice, and I developed three overarching goals:

1. Students will learn the rights protected by the Bill of Rights.

2. Students will learn how to argue effectively.

3. Students will become motivated to be active, engaged citizens.

We started the semester by discussing the underlying tension between individual liberties and community values and spent one week learning how to argue, using a book called *How to Win Every Argument* by Nicholas Capaldi (1999), which I had stumbled across at Barnes and Noble. We practiced every day with small discussions (like the neo-Nazi free speech one), learning how to use emotion and analogy, and when evidence and legal precedent were required.

After the introductory weeks, the class was built around formal debates, which took place on Fridays throughout the semester between teams of two or three students. All readings, lectures, and daily assignments were connected to the debates, so if we were approaching a student debate on physician-assisted suicide, for example, class materials would include lecture notes with a time line and stories about Karen Ann Quinlan and Nancy Cruzan; a *60 Minutes* video about Dr. Jack Kevorkian; the text of the Oregon Death with Dignity Act; and small-group case studies of individuals like Terri Schiavo (whose husband fought to remove her feeding tube) and Joni Eareckson Tada (who was paralyzed by a diving accident and wanted to commit suicide, but later became an activist against the "right to die").

The students read these personal stories and laws, watched videos, and learned about precedents. We did most of this work in class, to prevent the problem of unprepared students.

On debate day, two teams of students formally argued with each other before the class, presenting five-to-seven-minute arguments, three-to-five-minute impromptu rebuttals to their opponents' points, and concluding statements. The rest of the students were encouraged to ask questions and add their own insights. (See a sample debate outline in Appendix B, Chapter 4, Sample 1, available online at sten.pub/beatboredom.)

"It was fun," Alex Wald says. "In high school, you don't often have a chance to teach the class on your own. It's not like we were teaching the class, but for that specific subject, we were super well versed, and I was super-confident that I had a good grasp on what the major things were to know."

In his debate on physician-assisted suicide, Alex recalls, "We had to be thoughtful when we used numbers or percentages of things." The opposing team threw out a number—nearly six hundred deaths under Oregon's law—and his team responded by putting it in context. "Ninety-nine percent of people in this scenario don't choose death."

Anna Brockway, a former student who also debated in favor of physician-assisted suicide in a different year, remembers it as an eye-opening experience (personal interview, December 28, 2016). "One of the arguments we used was economic, the cost argument," Anna says. "There were some people who just couldn't hear that. I was surprised at how deeply they couldn't hear it and how emotional that debate suddenly became."

By the end of the semester, after learning about and debating a host of legal and constitutional issues, the students were skilled at preparing and presenting arguments, as well as carefully listening to the opposing side and rebutting their points. Perhaps more important, they cared deeply about a wide variety of judicial and political topics, which continued to surface in the news. Civil Liberties students e-mailed me to continue the conversation years later when Dr. Kevorkian went to prison, when the Supreme Court legalized same-sex marriage, when several states legalized marijuana.

Although Civil Liberties allowed me to build a class around discussion and debate, teachers don't need to use this strategy every day to implement it. My AP Microeconomics and AP Macroeconomics courses are not discussion-based, not the way Civil Liberties was, but we still take time for students to talk with each other about economic issues. AP Micro students have almost weekly online discussions on questions like *Is scarcity real? Does new research on incentives—showing that increased pay does not improve performance—contradict basic economic theory? Is Google a monopoly, and if so should it be regulated?*

This helps build relevance in the course, so economics is not simply a series of graphs and equations. In AP Macro, discussions emerge throughout the semester, as students start to question the use of government spending to stimulate the economy, whether government unemployment statistics are misleading, whether trade and globalization are beneficial. When we talk about income inequality, I show visual representations of the difference between the median family income of $55,000 (a pile of $100 bills a few inches tall) and $50 billion (a pile of $100 bills five times the height of Mount Everest). The students immediately have questions and comments.

"Does that mean people shouldn't be able to earn that much? What if they worked hard and started a business, like Bill Gates?"

"But even if you work hard, why should anyone have that much money? You can't even spend it!"

"So who should have it? That doesn't mean it should go to the government."

"Why can't lower-paid workers be paid a little bit more?"

I gently steer the conversation by pointing out what conservative and liberal economists say—some would respond that innovators take risks, drive economic growth, and deserve the rewards, while others would argue that severe inequality is destabilizing—and asking students to think about which values are most important to them. *Should we be concerned only with freedom and opportunity, or should we care about economic equality?*

Teachers can also use the principles of effective discussion and debate to make even routine classroom conversations more substantive. If you have time for only a two- or three-minute reflection before moving on to a new topic, you can still ask open-ended review questions. If my macroeconomics class has just finished learning about theories of international trade, I could do a typical check for understanding by asking,

- Why do we trade?

- What is comparative advantage?

- Who gains from voluntary trade?

I would be looking for very specific answers to these questions, such as "because trade makes both partners better off," "producing the good for which you have a lower opportunity cost," and "both parties." But I could elevate the conversation by instead asking

- If both parties gain from trade, why do some people oppose it?

- Are their arguments valid?

- If a nation doesn't have a comparative advantage in producing cars, is there any reason to produce rather than import cars?

These questions do not lead to just one response; instead, they challenge students to consider multiple points of view and formulate opinions. If one student offers an answer, I can encourage others to respond without evaluating whether the answer is "right" or "wrong." In a class where students are reluctant to answer, I often ask them to discuss at their tables instead of with the larger group, and I circulate to listen in.

WHAT ARE THE CHALLENGES OF USING DISCUSSION AND DEBATE?

One reason teachers don't use discussion and debate is a belief that the current climate of Common Core State Standards and high-stakes testing requires lecture and repetition and makes this kind of open-ended learning impossible. Although it may seem daunting to implement a course like Civil Liberties in today's standards-driven curricula, it can still be done.

Robin Moten's courses—both her "Flex" (which meets Michigan's English and social studies standards) and more traditional English classes—all incorporate regular seminar discussions. At Arete, where Mary Chin teaches math, classes in every subject area are designed with discussion as a core principle, and the students manage to learn calculus, read Aristotle, and master Newton's Laws.

Paula McAvoy and Diana Hess (2014) of the Spencer Foundation argue that the Common Core literacy standards encourage exactly these kinds of programs and courses. They describe a Midwestern school they called "Adams High," which requires all seniors to participate in an American Government course modeled on the legislative process. Every student posts to online discussion boards; every student takes a turn at chairing classroom meetings; and every student writes bills, discusses them in committee, and deliberates in a full congressional session. McAvoy and Hess describe this course not as an example of rebellion against standards, but as an example of how to meet current literacy requirements.

Teachers can also find support for using discussion and debate in standards recommended by the National Council for Teaching Mathematics Standards (NCTM), the National Council of Teachers of English (NCTE), the National Council for the Social Studies (NCSS), and the National Research Council's *Framework for K–12 Science Education*. Discussion and debate are not merely add-ons to a course, but fundamental to what we are trying to teach our students today.

Another barrier to implementing classroom discussions is a fear that students won't prepare for or know how to engage in discussion. Nearly every teacher has had the experience of trying to ignite a discussion and finding students unwilling to speak up. One colleague who taught Civil Liberties with me for several years regularly complained that his students "just don't care about their constitutional rights." But there are a number of ways we can prepare students, train them for meaningful discussions, and make them care.

- **Teach students how to discuss.** Our students do not know how to participate in discussions any more than they know how to write an essay, conduct a science experiment, or give a speech. We need to teach discussion skills explicitly in our courses, by describing argument strategies, letting students read sample arguments, and giving them repeated practice with discussion, either orally or using technology. We can help this process by starting with small discussions that don't require extensive reading and preparation.

- **Use "cold-calling" early in the semester to get students used to talking in class.** I call on students by name starting on the first day of class; I don't wait for them to volunteer. After they have spoken once, it's easier for them to speak up a second and third time. One study found that participation in class discussions increased from fewer than half in classrooms with little cold-calling to more than 90 percent in high cold-calling sections.

- **Encourage students to write before they talk.** My Civil Liberties students always answered a few reflection questions on a reading before we began discussing, so that everyone would have time to process their thoughts before anyone started talking. This helps students commit to their own ideas, rather than being influenced by the loudest voices. Online discussions are also an option to consider because they create a safe opportunity for quieter students. I have found many introverts are far more willing to contribute—and to contribute extensively—when they write their views online.

- **Build relationships in class.** Students report that they talk more in classes where they feel like they know each other and know the teacher, so building in story-sharing early on can pave the way for deep, content-related discussions later. Alex Wald said the close relationships in Civil Liberties class were critical to creating a trusting, open environment: "It's kind of a rare thing where people are OK with being wrong in a class in high school or college. . . . It felt to me like a lot of that class was kind of an intellectual play space. I never felt like I was being appraised."

- **Establish norms for discussion early on.** Once a classroom culture is established, it is difficult to change, so lecturing for six weeks and then suddenly calling on students to discuss will result in an uncomfortable silence. In addition to creating a norm of discussion itself, it's critical to encourage students to think about how they talk to each other. In Civil Liberties, we talked about the importance of actively listening to each other, showing respect for others' experiences and opinions, working to include everyone, and disagreeing tactfully. I also frequently reminded students that there is much in our personal lives that others do not know. When we talked about physician-assisted suicide, I encouraged them to think: *What if a classmate's parent was in a coma? What if a classmate's parent had committed suicide?* When we talked about abortion, I stressed that they knew very little about each other's families or personal stories, including experiences with adoption, pregnancy, and rape.

- **Support unpopular positions.** If a student expresses an unpopular view, even one you do not agree with, it is important to help that student feel supported and appreciated. If no one is expressing a particular view, the teacher may need to play devil's advocate and speak up for the unrepresented minority. That means really knowing and understanding the issue from all sides. I had to learn the evidence and arguments for both sides of every issue in Civil Liberties, so that I could feel comfortable in this role. Although I am generally in favor of gun control, I can argue that the Second Amendment is what stands between us and a dictatorship. I can also argue for and against school prayer, abortion, and the death penalty. (In many cases, I found my own opinions evolving and changing.)

Sometimes students do resist engaging in discussion and debate, even in the best circumstances. One reason is that students are used to being spoon-fed information, especially in quantitative subjects, and change is scary for them as well.

Reluctance to deal with controversy is another reason teachers find discussion and debate challenging. Many social studies teachers found it safer and more comfortable to show students a PowerPoint about the Electoral College than to encourage students to ask questions or share their opinions about presidential candidates Hillary Clinton and Donald Trump in 2016. If we try to keep discussion and debate to safe topics, though, they won't work. No one wants to discuss a bland question like *Is health care important?* Of course health care is important. A question like *Should the government provide health care to all citizens?* is more controversial, but that's what makes it more engaging. John Dewey called controversy "the gadfly of thought," and he was right.

Perhaps the biggest challenge to using discussion and debate is teacher self-confidence. Many teachers are comfortable and experienced with the Initiation-Response-Evaluation system they are using—and not comfortable or experienced with monitoring and scaffolding a student discussion. Teachers need the opportunity to watch expert colleagues lead discussions and also experience meaningful discussions during professional development. Fostering discussion and debate is a skill, just as participating in discussion and debate is a skill, and both teachers and students need practice to become experts.

TIPS FOR TEACHERS

How do I get started if I have never used open-ended discussion or debate?

- Use "cold-calling" in class—calling on all students at random, rather than seeking volunteers—to make sure all students have practice speaking in class. Make sure you use soft questions early in the semester, like *How would you describe this figure?* or *What is an example of a substitute good?* to build students' confidence in participating.

- Create a culture of discussion where every student knows his or her opinion will be listened to and valued—both by stating this principle explicitly and adhering to it in class. When students do voice dissenting opinions, listen and validate them with your words as well as attentive, respectful body language. Step in when needed to stop the louder voices from dominating.

- Develop open-ended questions to use during lessons, and give students time to respond and reflect before you follow with a comment or additional questions.

- Find topics that spark student interest, and give students time to discuss them (or online opportunities) with minimal intervention or guidance. In Marcus Peterson's (personal interview, August 9, 2016) support class in New York, students wanted to talk about school resource officers, so he let them. When the Newtown shooting happened, my students were in Government class, and we began processing their fears and opinions right away.

- Do not state your opinion on an ambiguous or controversial topic, whenever possible. Most of my students never knew where I stood on abortion, same-sex marriage, gun control, or a host of other issues, which made it easier for them to speak up. They knew I would offer support to whichever view was less popular.

How can I build on my use of discussion and debate to encourage better participation and deeper learning?

- Record your class during a discussion or debate and watch later to evaluate your role and student participation. Ask yourself:

  ○ Are students talking to each other or performing for me? In other words, are they looking to me for validation of their responses? Are they trying to provide a right answer?

  ○ Am I intervening only as necessary, or do I continue to act as the "expert"?

  ○ Are all students participating, or only a few? If only a few are speaking, develop strategies to include more students. Encourage student leaders to draw their classmates into discussion; divide students into smaller discussion groups; allow more time for reflection before starting the discussion.

- Ask students for feedback about class discussion and debate on an anonymous evaluation form, and see if they feel comfortable sharing their opinions in your class. If not, why not?

- Think broadly about concepts that could be taught through discussion and debate. These strategies are not only useful for political discussion or poetry analysis; they are also useful for group problem solving in any subject. Some teachers use Twitter to get students to brainstorm hypotheses in science class. In my psychology class, students discuss how to define learning in small groups, then post their answers to an online forum, so we can discuss all of them as a class.

- Take on a controversial issue in your subject area and prepare students to see all sides of the issue before a discussion. Give them plenty of time and leeway, so they understand that you trust them to carry the discussion. Afterward, have a meta-conversation with students about what they learned and what you could do differently. Robin Moten had an open discussion about violence and police shootings with her senior English class at Seaholm High School, and her diverse group of students had a deep conversation (classroom observation, September 23, 2016). Here's a brief excerpt:

  - *"There's nothing you can teach us that's going to guarantee our safety."*

  - *"This is difficult to talk about–should we talk about the shootings versus rioting? Could it be seen as unfair if you talk about one versus the other?"*

  - *"The Orlando [nightclub] shooting really got to me."*

  - *"They all should get to you."*

  In the meta-conversation afterward, Moten asked students what they wanted from her as a teacher and how she could help them process what was happening in Orlando, in Oklahoma, in North Carolina. "The question is what do you do about it in school? What do I do? What's my responsibility to my black students? What's my responsibility to my white students? . . . What is our responsibility to Seaholm High School to create a space where you guys can have these conversations?" The students told her they valued the chance to talk. "I don't see any teachers beyond a select few bringing this up," one said. "We have a Birmingham [local community] bubble. I feel like that's a problem."

How will I assess and know if it's effective?

- Use the same assessments you are using now to compare the effectiveness of teaching content with debate and discussion.

- Develop rubrics to assess student participation–for example, award one point for contributing to the discussion but two points for adding a question, responding to another student, or quoting from text.

- Use postdiscussion reflection papers to allow students to share what they have learned. Many will tell you they can't stop discussing issues, once they start.

5

PROBLEM-BASED LEARNING: LET STUDENTS STRUGGLE WITH REAL (UNSOLVED) PROBLEMS

"If we cover Nebraska with solar cells, do we have enough power to actually alleviate our energy usage? Would that be enough to replace oil?"

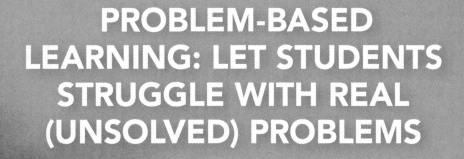

Mike Lampert's physics students had already learned about watts and joules. They had calculated how many watts they could sustain walking up the stairs and measured how many joules the school uses in electricity each month— counting lights classroom by classroom.

They had also ventured outside with cups of water to measure the energy output of the sun, calculating the rise in temperature over time.

Now it was time to answer the "Nebraska Question."

"I give each kid a solar cell. They measure the area of the cell and the open circuit voltage and short circuit amperage," he explains (personal interview, June 16, 2016). "They calculate the percentage of energy converted from sunlight to electrical. . . . After that, they build a solar car from Legos and a motor and several cells. As part of their report, they have to measure the efficiency of their cars.

"They must finally decide if we have enough power from the sun to replace fossil fuels.

"Encouraging students to explore these kinds of open-ended, high-level, real-world questions is an engaging way to get them to learn science," Lampert says.

Unlike many American high school students, who are turned off to science by the time they reach ninth grade, his students at West Salem High School in Oregon enjoy it. They also build electronic circuits to measure the ripeness of watermelons. They create artistic pulley systems. They travel to the Oregon coast to listen to the ocean with sonar receivers. They build rockets from construction paper, then insert engines. Every day is something different.

"I engage them with questions, new things they haven't seen," he says.

"The lesson stays longer when you have to figure it out yourself, and you have to struggle," says Casey Chaffin, one of his students (personal interview, December 20, 2016).

WHAT IS PROBLEM-BASED LEARNING?

Most of what we teach high school students is established factual knowledge: solved problems, defined terms, proven theorems, and the outcomes of wars, experiments, social movements, and court cases. Mostly what we ask students to do is memorize these facts—or correctly apply our established models, theories, rules, and precedents.

Problem-Based Learning (PBL) turns that type of conventional teaching and learning on its head. Instead of telling students answers, we ask them complex, real-world questions:

What's the best way to improve K–12 education in the United States?

Should states and cities spend taxpayer funds on sports stadiums?

What could be causing a patient to have an elevated heart rate?

What's the strongest design for a bridge?

How can we relieve California's water shortage?

None of these questions has an easy or defined answer—*we* can't even answer them—which makes them a whole lot more interesting to teenagers. They get to look for their own solutions and, in the process, acquire the skills and knowledge we want them to have. Lampert has a pretty good idea what his students will learn when they work on the Nebraska Question, but he doesn't hand them a solution. "By posing a problem-based question, I feel they learn the standards in a more subtle and indirect way," he says.

Another one of his problems involves building bridges. In 2013, the Skagit River Bridge in Washington State collapsed, so Lampert shows his freshman physical science class a video of the collapse and challenges them to build the strongest bridge they can design out of thin sticks and glue. They can work on them at home, with their families' help, but they have very little instruction about engineering design. "There was no, 'Here's how you make a bridge,'" Casey Chaffin says. "'This long and this tall,' that was basically it."

When the students return to school with their wide variety of bridges, they are all put on display. The students vote for the ones they predict will hold the most weight. They are graded not on their own bridge, but on their ability to identify what makes a bridge strong. Then they test the bridges by hanging weights on them until they collapse.

Casey, who was never very interested in math or science, loved it. When she started out, she wasn't thinking about net force or torque, but she learned them intuitively through the process. "I remember being really proud of myself because my bridge held more than I thought it was going to. I realized I could do things that I didn't think I could do. I consider myself a writer, not a science-oriented person," Casey says.

Lampert, who says bridge building is a popular assignment among science teachers, is always impressed by the students' designs—and what they learn. "This is how we teach statics," he says.

Problem-Based Learning was first developed for medical training in the 1970s in response to findings that medical students were having trouble retaining all of the facts they were taught in lectures and case studies. In this method, sometimes called PBL (but distinct from project-based learning), medical students are given complex problems and assigned to work in collaborative groups to determine what information they need, what skills they must develop, and what solution or treatment to recommend. The medical students who learn by this method develop better cognitive skills and retain more factual knowledge than students trained in traditional methods. Johannes Strobel, now a professor at the University of Missouri, and Angela Van Barneveld, an instructor at Purdue University, conducted a "meta-synthesis" of the research on PBL and determined that it is "significantly more effective than traditional instruction to train competent and skilled practitioners and to promote long-term retention of knowledge and skills" (Strobel and Van Barneveld 2009, 55).

After this success, Problem-Based Learning emerged as a teaching strategy in lots of disciplines, including engineering, science, history, math, statistics, economics, and even teacher training. John Savery (2006), an education professor and advocate for PBL, says problem-based lessons should include all of the following criteria:

- Students should bear the responsibility for their own learning. (Lampert's students were responsible for learning how to design and build their bridges; he did not tell them how.)

- The teacher should act as a facilitator, rather than the source of knowledge. (Again, Lampert posed the problem and provided tools; he didn't tell them how it should be done.)

- Learning should incorporate multiple subjects. (Bridge building includes physics, engineering, math, and art.)

- The problems should be ill-structured and messy, like real-world problems. (Building strong bridges is clearly a real-world problem, especially when we have seen them collapse.)

- Students should collaborate and communicate in group problem solving. (Students built the bridges with their families, and also collaborated in evaluating them when they returned to school.)

- Students should share and reflect on what they have learned. (Students voted on bridge designs and discussed what worked best.)

Problem-Based Learning can be used in many different subjects, but it doesn't work for every kind of problem. Some problems are too simple for a PBL inquiry: *What would happen to California's water shortage if authorities raised the price of water?* (Basic supply and demand analysis tells us people would use less water, helping alleviate the shortage.) Others are too complex: *Why does California experience drought?* (A true exploration of this question requires professional-level knowledge of atmospheric science, as well as the history of California's convoluted water management system.) An appropriate PBL inquiry might be *Using economic analysis, what is the most viable current solution to California's water shortage?* (More on that later.)

The best kinds of problems are ones that require students to learn and apply both theory and knowledge, but also allow creativity and the exploration of multiple solutions (Jonassen and Hung 2008). For example:

- Diagnosis-solution problems: *Why is the patient sick? Why are the fish dying?*

- Decision-making problems: *What's the best use of vacant lots in a city neighborhood? What business could we design to help senior citizens with technology?*

- Policy problems: *How should we fix our education system? Is an alternative school the best setting for a struggling student?*

Although Problem-Based Learning is a very specific way of structuring lessons—and it usually can't be done in one class period or for one isolated concept—we can use some of the principles of PBL to design smaller-scale inquiry lessons as well. We can let our students build math or economics knowledge by solving progressively more challenging problems or let our psychology students analyze their peers' sleep habits, to see if they are suffering sleep deprivation.

What's important is that students learn to ask questions and figure out their own solutions, rather than merely memorizing and applying what we, "the experts," tell them.

WHY USE PROBLEM-BASED LEARNING?

Our students are tired of being asked, year after year, to answer hundreds of boring factual-recall questions with no obvious relevance to their lives. *What is outside the door of the prison where Hester Prynne is kept? Which European country was Napoleon unable to conquer? What form of RNA carries instructions from the nucleus to the ribosome?*

It's hard to focus on these details when your mind is really on *How am I going to get my homework done when I have to work late? Are my parents going to be mad about my grades? Why won't my car start?* If we can engage students' minds with interesting, realistic, real-world problems, we at least have a fighting chance of keeping their attention on learning.

Eric Toshalis, an expert in defiant student behavior, says even the most difficult students respond better when we actively engage their imaginations in solving interesting problems. Students are naturally inquisitive, but they are also suspicious of prepackaged answers, he says. "If classroom texts yield only adult-sanctioned interpretations, if science labs are predetermined, if math problems can only be solved in one way, and if opinions about historical events are constrained to whatever the experts declare, adolescents will divert their imaginations away from academics and into activities where they themselves can flourish" (2015, 79).

So we need to give students problems where their thinking matters, where their insights are genuinely meaningful. *How would you improve your school? What's the best use for this vacant lot in your neighborhood? How can we persuade teenagers to get more sleep?*

Solving real problems is what adults do at work, at home, in the political realm—in short, in their real lives—every day. So even if the problems are a bit removed from students' immediate lives, such as *How can we save the walleye population in Lake Mille Lacs (Minnesota)?* teenagers buy in to solving problems that an adult might actually tackle in a real job. Look to what scientists, entrepreneurs, political leaders, educators, journalists, economists, and business managers do every day, and we should have plenty of engaging material.

For example, consider this question: *What change in the American K–12 education system would result in the most cost-effective improvement in student outcomes?* This was the topic for the Ninth District Federal Reserve Essay Contest, which I assigned to my seventy AP Macroeconomics students in spring of 2016. I can't think of a much more relevant question—or one that would be more engaging to a group of high school students. Are adults trying to answer it? Definitely. And if there's one thing teenagers have strong opinions about, it's what is wrong with their schools.

What is the right answer? Charter schools? Private school vouchers? A longer school day? A later start time? Year-round school? Desegregation? Less state testing? My students (mostly fourteen- and fifteen-year-olds) struggled a bit with how to approach this broad question, but the struggle made it engaging. They realized they had to understand the problem better before they could start analyzing the costs and benefits of possible solutions.

"Going into it I felt a little blind; I didn't know what to research," says Libby Fleming (personal interview, October 31, 2016), a former AP Macroeconomics student. For most school writing assignments, there are strict guidelines, rubrics, and steps to follow, she said. "I spent a lot of time researching just to come up with a topic."

One of my students came across the idea of "Lesson Study," which is used in Japan, Germany, and Finland to improve and refine individual lesson plans. He found that in Chicago, this strategy has led to improved test scores. Many students wrote about pushing back school start times—our school day starts at the brutal hour of 7:25 a.m.—citing study after study showing better attendance, alertness, problem solving, and grades.

Libby ended up writing her essay about year-round school, and she found a lot of evidence in favor of eliminating the long summer break (even though she doesn't really want to). She found that a large portion of the achievement gap between white and nonwhite students originates over the summer, when disadvantaged children lose ground. "The loss of material over the summer is so great that American K–12 teachers typically use the first month of each school year to re-teach what was lost," Libby wrote.

The question was interesting enough to her that she talked about it at home, even with family friends who were over for dinner. One suggested she write about technology and how students can learn from educational websites like the Khan Academy, but Libby found herself more interested in the scheduling issue. *What would it be like to attend year-round school? Would it really make a difference?* "There aren't many schools that follow the year-long calendar, so there wasn't too much information," she says. "But one of the articles was talking about the difference between disadvantaged students and advantaged students, then I researched that more, so that helped guide my essay."

Libby's final paper was exemplary—she won the essay contest and a paid summer internship at the Federal Reserve Bank. But the learning was not easy or routine. Nor was it what she expected when she signed up for an economics class. "I definitely felt challenged when writing the essay, but I think challenge is good," she says. "That essay made me a little bit stronger of a writer and a researcher. . . . I'm glad we had to do it." (See Libby's winning essay, Chapter 5, Sample 1, in the appendix.)

Another complicated issue that's highly engaging to students is city planning. Ethan Cherin (personal interview, December 16, 2016), who teaches economics and philosophy at St. Paul Central High School, involved his IB Economics students in the Urban Land Institute's (ULI) UrbanPlan program in 2016 (http://minnesota.uli.org/programs-and-events/urbanplan/). In this project, students work in teams of five as urban planners, and they are given a "Request for Proposal" from Yorktown, an imaginary city, to redevelop a blighted area of five or six blocks. The Urban Land Institute sets specific criteria for the proposal—for example, the project must generate a certain level of tax revenue for the city as well as profit for the developer (just like real life)—and provides a wealth of background information including constituent letters, parking requirements, and absorption rates. The students draft a proposal, create a model using Legos, calculate the economic impact using spreadsheets, and present their proposals to a panel of judges, including local landscape architects.

Cherin's students describe the project as "very hard," "unfamiliar," "a struggle," "a puzzle that didn't really have a definite answer," and "really professional."

"It gave us a good insight into the real world," says Ian Heegaard.

Ian and his group developed their mission statement first. They wanted to create a modern feel, to blend the new buildings with the existing downtown area, to be inclusive, and to offer opportunities for people who live nearby. Then they started arguing about the details (group interview, January 5, 2017).

"I wanted to get rid of the homeless shelter," Ian explains. "It brought crime to the neighborhood; we could use the space for other stuff."

Tori Garvey shakes her head.

"People don't want to have stuff by a homeless shelter," Ian repeats. But he relents: "Also, we didn't want to be people who kick out the homeless shelter."

"Looking at the letters given to us—two requested having the homeless shelter," Tori says. "But also on a more social level, I think it's important."

"Part of our mission statement was providing an inclusive community," Isaac Ash adds.

"I get what Ian was saying," says Skylah Thao. "I tried to put it in real-life perspective. No one wants to live by a homeless shelter or go by a homeless shelter. But our vision statement was that we didn't want to exclude anybody.

When we got feedback on our project, they said if we talked about our personal opinion more, it would seem like we were being real about it. Me, personally, it felt like it was more right to keep the homeless shelter."

As a compromise, they decided to move the homeless shelter to a location near a church.

A lot of the urban planning process was trial and error, and they made mistakes along the way, like overestimating absorption rates and misreading the revenue requirements. The first time through, Isaac says, "We plugged it in the spreadsheet, and it made like -20 percent for our investors. It was because we had three luxury condos and we didn't realize at that point that only one or one-and-a-half would fill up within the ten years. We had an empty luxury condo."

They also had to consider a lot of moving parts. "There were a lot of parking requirements," Skylah says. "Every time we added a new building, we had to not only think about how the residents felt but how big it is and how much parking it would take up."

"We had a bad habit of overestimating space and cost," Tori adds.

In the end, the ULI judges picked their proposal as the best one in their class. In just three weeks, they had developed a viable redevelopment plan that earned its required return. The students describe UrbanPlan as an amazing, authentic learning experience that made them rethink what they see when they walk around St. Paul—and learn terms like *opportunity cost*, *trade-offs*, *interest rates*, *rate of return*, *absorption rates*, and a host of other concepts without even trying.

"You sit down with a test, and you're right or you're wrong, it's A or it's B," says Aidan Meekin. "It was still a matter of completing this and trying to get an A, but it felt like an open-ended puzzle you were able to put your own creative little twist on. It made it a lot more fun."

A puzzle. A challenge. A struggle. Students use the same words to describe all of these Problem-Based Learning activities. They're not easy, but they're definitely not dull. Another advantage of using problem-based activities is that students aren't restricted to solving problems we create. They start identifying, researching, and trying to solve problems of their own—something that's critically missing from much of our education system.

David Perkins, the author of *Making Learning Whole*, says learning to find problems is critical but was almost completely absent from his own education, even in his undergraduate and graduate studies at MIT, which made it very difficult for him to choose a dissertation topic. "I had never undertaken anything like a project or an open-ended investigation," he said. "The consequence was inevitable: I had a fierce battery of problem-solving skills and hardly any problem-finding skills" (2010, 26).

How will our future entrepreneurs choose which ventures to start or journalists decide which stories to report on or medical researchers decide which diseases to research if they don't know how to find or define problems for themselves?

In my AP Microeconomics course, after several years of assigning students funny, instructional music videos as their culminating course project (an idea I got from AP colleagues), I decided that they should be using their newly acquired economics skills to create a more meaningful capstone. For the past few years, they have worked in groups to research and write an economic analysis of a current issue or problem that interests them. Last year, students decided on these questions (among others):

> *Should airlines be required to pass fuel savings on to customers?*
>
> *Should Minnesota provide tax breaks for the new Minnesota United soccer stadium?*
>
> *Should we require humane treatment of food animals on factory farms?*
>
> *What should be done to lower the price of EpiPens?*
>
> *How should California deal with its water shortage?*

The students do background research to understand the nature and causes of their chosen problem, then analyze it using an economic lens. For example, they might analyze how monopoly power helped Mylan raise the price of EpiPens or how the tragedy of the commons contributed to California's water issues.

Abhi Vijayakumar, Solomon Shih, and Bryan Park, who analyzed California's water shortage for their project in fall 2016, say the process really made them think (group interviews, December 20, 2016, and January 11, 2017).

"It was more interesting than other class assignments because you're thinking about the solution on your own, and there's not a defined correct answer," Solomon says.

"We were kind of making our own assignment and then doing it," Abhi says. "Normative economics is fun. Understanding the issue—it's not like the models helped us understand immediately, but the models helped us understand what they should do and what they are trying."

While they were working on the project, they had a lot of lively debates as well as frustration, trying to understand such a complex issue, with so many causes and complicating factors.

One morning, a few weeks before the project was due, Abhi and Solomon were working together in my classroom on how to describe and analyze possible solutions. One solution they considered was reallocating water that has been dedicated for the environment, and letting consumers and farmers use it.

"So, we'll say 'reallocate the water to the citizens,'" Abhi proposes while typing.

"Sure, that sounds fancy," Solomon says.

"Allow environmental water to be reallocated to . . . I guess it would go to both? Instead of 10 percent [consumers] and 40 percent [agriculture], it would go to 20 percent and 80 percent?" Abhi continues.

"Don't you want to do a 'but' too? But it will kill the environment?" Solomon asks.

"Yes, but we should do more positives first," Abhi replies. "The supply of water would increase to eliminate the shortage without any increases in price or possible decreases in price."

"It wouldn't change what the farmers produce or anything."

"Yeah, it wouldn't change production because they're still producing. It would eliminate the shortage in the water distribution system, but it wouldn't increase the price."

"It would solve the problem without affecting the current market. The other solutions are 'farmers have to change their crops,' or 'we have to reduce consumption,'" Solomon says.

"Yes, the other solutions would have to change behavior, and people don't like that," Abhi concludes.

A few minutes later, they circle back to the drawbacks of this plan.

"If you take the water out, it could cause desertification," Solomon suggests.

"But far away from where you live," Abhi says.

"It's going to cause problems, but in the future."

"In the long term. But the person there doesn't care about the long term."

"But that's still a downside—" Solomon starts.

"It's a downside overall to society," Abhi interjects, "like a negative externality."

In these brief exchanges, Abhi and Solomon are building their understanding of how to analyze problems using economics, and they are using and reviewing multiple key economic concepts: *allocation, supply and demand, shortages, prices, social costs and negative externalities,* and *short-term versus long-term decision making.* More important, they are talking about these concepts as if they matter.

Ultimately, the group recommended a combination of policies—but not reallocating environmental water to household and farm use.

"They should increase the price of water for farmers and use that money to subsidize substitute crops that require less intensive water usage," Abhi explains. "It would prioritize water for civilians. Farmers' quantity demanded would be lower, and farmers would be further encouraged to go after other crops. We decided not to go after environmental because of the long-term consequences for the entire state." (See the group's final project in Appendix B, Chapter 5, Sample 2, available online at sten.pub/beatboredom.)

Problem-Based Learning like this doesn't just motivate students; it actually changes the way they learn. Daniel Schwartz and John Bransford, professors in Vanderbilt University's Learning Technology Center, explain that our brains work differently when we are problem solving. When people grapple with a real problem, their brains are primed to learn relevant facts and theories. They are literally hungry for information that will help them find a solution. If we teach a solution first, as we usually do, the learning is out of context, superficial, and easily forgotten.

"When telling occurs without readiness, the primary recourse for students is to treat the new information as ends to be memorized rather than as tools to help them perceive and think" (Schwartz and Bransford 1998, 477).

When students are hungry for information, they can learn just about anything. Listen to this earlier exchange between Abhi and Solomon, when they were trying to simply understand California's existing water policies (classroom observation, December 20, 2016). Abhi is in the school library googling "How many people have been fined for water overuse in California?" while Solomon is next to him, scrolling through an online 2,300-page document of California water statutes, wishing he could find a summary page (or use Wikipedia instead).

"What I know is that they cut up the Colorado River so each state gets a certain amount," Solomon says.

"Like smaller water flowing past your house, I know you can use some, but there is an excessive use policy," Abhi adds. "Solly, anything they think is unreasonable, they fine you."

A few seconds later, Abhi laughs. "Solly, I found the numbers. Each unit of water is thirty dollars. Do you know what the units are?"

"I was researching another kind of water law."

"The riparian one?"

"Yes, where if you own the land the water is on, you can use the water."

I never assigned them to study (or even define) riparian water laws or fines for overuse (or #droughtshaming, which also came up), but they were curious, so they pursued it for themselves. My role was mainly to guide them by asking questions on their drafts—like, *Do farmers have rights to the water? Who owns it?* (which I asked on their first draft)—prompting them to look for more details.

This shift from extrinsic motivation—learning because a teacher will reward you—to intrinsic motivation—learning because it's part of an interesting puzzle—was also revealed during PBL research in Hong Kong. In one middle school, a teacher and researcher introduced Problem-Based Learning to students who had been taught only by lecture and rote memorization. In traditional lectures, motivation was tied to the teacher's charisma, they found, but in PBL, "the students seem to be motivated by their own curiosity when presented with interesting problems" (Wong and Day 2008, 637).

The learning in PBL also becomes more purposeful and holistic. Students learn to research because they need to find information; they learn to write because they need to communicate; they learn data analysis because they need to read a spreadsheet. Will Tjernlund, a former student (and now entrepreneur), says he wishes he could have designed his entire high school education around solving problems meaningful to him (personal interview, December 6, 2016). He would have learned critical skills, he says, in a way that made sense to him. "Let me start a company," he said. "I'm sure I will be going to the English teachers asking for help on copywriting and going to the math teachers to help me figure out profitability and figure out accounting."

A final reason for using Problem-Based Learning is that it teaches 21st century skills such as critical thinking, collaboration, and communication, along with content knowledge.

The National Research Council (NRC) and the National Council of Teachers of Mathematics (NCTM) both promote Problem-Based Learning in all levels of science and math classes, arguing that PBL engages all students in a more experimental approach to learning and reasoning for themselves.

José Garcia, a teacher in Greene County, North Carolina, has seen that happen. He started using Problem-Based Learning in his middle school science classes in 2009. By 2012, when test scores in his classes were taking off, he was asked to take over as STEM coordinator for the district. The Greene Central High School STEM program he created now serves two hundred students—one-fourth of the school's student body—and they are seeing a positive impact on students' science and math achievement, presentation skills, collaboration skills, reading, and writing (personal interview, December 21, 2016).

In the STEM program, instruction is organized around "grand challenges" (based on the National Academy of Engineering Grand Challenges—http://www.engineeringchallenges.org/) that are both global and interdisciplinary. Students develop a project, and teachers set the parameters and rubrics. "They take a look at a problem that a specific country is having—for example, Japan, Germany, or Brazil—they figure out a solution to that problem for that country, and they develop a product," Garcia explains. "Some of them have very good ideas. . . . I think we're very close in some of our students to patenting the ideas."

Science, math, social studies, Spanish, English, and even creative writing classes and electives are incorporated. In one Grand Challenge, students designed a new forensics kit that could have helped police solve the Jack the Ripper murders. In another, students engineered a way for Romeo to get Juliet down from her balcony quickly without getting caught.

"Students are finding relevance to all the content that they are learning," Garcia says. "They really are focusing and paying attention to their classes."

Marco Garcia, one of the students in the STEM program, says that in the past four years he has figured out how to make paper fireproof, created a portable microscope, and worked on a way to keep food fresh in the desert, among countless other challenges (personal interview, February 23, 2017). When I spoke with him, he was working with a team on how to incorporate a camera and AV output into clothing. One of the biggest differences between traditional instruction and the PBL program is that teachers expect students to find their own answers. "You're motivated to go find the answer for yourself, rather than them just telling you and you not learning it," Marco says. "You're always doing something; you're constantly moving. You're never just sitting there bored."

José Garcia says the improved test scores did not show up in the first year. "The first year I did it, right around April, I panicked a little bit," he says. "I hadn't given a chapter test or anything like that. I was relying heavily on formative assessments and Problem-Based Learning."

That year, his state test scores were in the red, and his teacher proficiency score was at -2. (North Carolina's EVAAS [Education Value-Added Assessment System] evaluation model compares students' expected growth scores to what actually happens, and a teacher's effectiveness is rated between -16 and +10.) The second year, his score moved to -0.4, meaning his students were close to expected growth.

When he left the classroom after four years of fully embracing Problem-Based Learning, he was +9. "I had probably my lowest group of students, and that year I ended up with 100 percent proficiency, and all the students scored at the highest level on the state science test. We're talking about students who were basically not even supposed to have 3s [proficient] or 4s [above proficient]."

His school, which serves a 30 percent migrant population, went from 32 percent proficiency in science to 64 percent, an amazing turnaround. "We have less behavior issues, and the teachers are enjoying teaching this way," Garcia says.

HOW DO YOU INCLUDE PBL IN YOUR INSTRUCTION?

Garcia's interdisciplinary STEM program within Greene Central High School is one way to incorporate PBL. Greene County's program has been so successful that they plan to keep growing it to serve more students. In order to keep succeeding as they expand—especially with new staff—all the PBL STEM teachers meet early each summer for training and curriculum development, so that everyone understands how to design and teach a well-constructed PBL course.

"A lot of times they're being told to teach this way, but they don't get the training that's required," he says. "Teachers think they are doing hands on, but there's really no content. Or if they do content, they're leaving out the life skills."

More common is organizing a single course around Problem-Based Learning. Kelly Gallagher (personal interview, October 13, 2016) has turned her anatomy/physiology course at Linden High School in New Jersey into a yearlong investigation of fictitious medical patients' symptoms, modeled on the book *Diagnosis for Classroom Success* (Maller 2013). At the beginning of the year, her students apply for "jobs" as interns at "Gallagher General

Hospital"—some will be surgical residents, others PhD candidates, social workers, or administrators. She hires them (assigning them to teams), and as they learn various parts of human anatomy, the students analyze tests on the eight patients. For example, once they have learned about the excretory system and urinary tract, they receive eight "urine samples" created by Gallagher. The students look at urinalysis results for each patient to identify dehydration, kidney damage, protein urea, or other abnormalities. The results go into the patients' medical charts, and at the end of the year each team of residents hypothesizes about each patient's condition using all of the test results.

"It really puts so much discovery on their end," Gallagher says. "They feel like they're finding out the information instead of just taking down notes and answering questions. Some kids get frustrated—What's the answer? Is it this? Could she have this?"

If students come up with the wrong diagnosis for some patients at the end, that's just part of the learning, Gallagher says. She is interested in the process—how students collect and analyze information and how they arrive at their conclusions. "I do periodic checks of their notes; I see that they've recorded results wrong," she says. "Sometimes I will fix it for them so they have the right information to move forward. Others, I make them suffer. I like to see them sweat and struggle—that's why you have to be focused [in class]. What would happen if you told somebody they were negative for HIV, and they were positive?"

Gallagher helps make sure that the one diagnosis the group presents to the rest of the class (wearing white lab coats, of course) is correct, so that no one is embarrassed. Very few students fail her class, and many end up interested in pursuing medical careers.

Another method for implementing PBL is to facilitate students doing their own research inquiries. Mike Lampert, the Oregon physics teacher, teaches an honors research course that encourages students to develop their own questions and pursue their own inquiries. Last year, one of his student groups developed a stove that cooks and creates electricity at the same time—a project they took to national science fairs.

Eleanor Fadely, one of Lampert's former students, took honors research during both her junior and senior years, and she got extensive experience developing her own research problems and trying to solve them (personal interview, December 23, 2016). Junior year, her team studied how to make concrete more environmentally friendly. Lampert wasn't an expert in concrete, but "he would make himself an expert in whatever field you were interested in doing research in," Eleanor says. In addition, she says, he would constantly boost the students' confidence. "Whenever I was struggling with a problem or struggling with my research, I would ask him for help. He would tell me, 'You can do this, I know you can.' . . . I think that if I hadn't had him as a teacher, I probably wouldn't be studying science now."

Courses in entrepreneurship and journalism can also serve as laboratories for Problem-Based Learning. The current trend in business schools and corporate America is the "Lean Startup" method of innovation, which basically involves identifying problems and working to develop viable (and profitable) solutions—and putting them out there quickly to test them. Traditional business plans focused on "Here's my idea and what I can do for you," but the new method focuses on "What do you need from me, and how can I best provide it?" That means student entrepreneurs are constantly doing PBL. (We'll look more at entrepreneurship in Chapter 8.)

Journalism students (and other writers and researchers) also need to learn how to find problems and evaluate solutions. Journalism teachers don't (or shouldn't) decide what stories should be covered; they rely on students to notice issues and talk about them. When Anna Brockway (personal interview, December 28, 2016) and Sisi Wei (personal interview, December 16, 2016) were editors on our high school newspaper, the *Viewer*, they became curious about why some students disappeared from our high school halls at Mounds View (MV) and went to the Area Learning Center (ALC) instead. They wanted to find out what this alternative school was really like, who went there, and what they did there. I helped them think about what kinds of questions to ask, what kind of data to gather, and whom to interview.

The girls went to the high school office and got an ALC referral form. "This form literally had, like, six check boxes—check if any of these categories describe you: drug user, pregnant, have failed a lot of classes," Anna recalls. "I remember the 'pregnant' one being really stark. If you qualify, you will be admitted. That was just mind-blowing to me, that that was the process they were using to determine who was being sent to the ALC."

After extensive reporting, Anna and Sisi framed their question this way: "The ALC: Is this alternative an equivalent to MV?" In their front-page story, they quoted students and faculty about their experiences at the ALC compared with Mounds View and tried to pin down whether the alternative school was an easy way out—or just an alternative. The answers were difficult to find, and they ended up without a conclusive resolution. "I spoke with two students who had both spent time at the ALC, one of whom had a very positive perspective, the other a very negative and critical perspective," Anna says.

Teachers can also use Problem-Based Learning as a way to structure a unit or research project, even in a mostly traditional course. In AP Microeconomics, the semesterlong study of a microeconomic question is one assignment, while the students also attend weekly seminars, participate in online discussions, and take tests. In AP Psychology, some lessons are designed as inquiries while others are taught by lecture, discussion, simulation, or more often a combination.

When we studied sleep and "states of consciousness" this year, my students spent a week working in collaborative groups on an inquiry into students' sleep habits, investigating the question *Do high school students get enough sleep?* They collected data on their own sleep habits and put it in a Google form, which then created a spreadsheet of about seventy students' sleep data, including bedtimes, total hours of sleep, caffeine intake, and number of times waking during the night. The students also read about the physiology of sleep and recommended sleep schedules, then produced PSAs or posters advising their peers about their sleep habits.

In one PSA, created by a group of three students, the voice-over starts, "It's common knowledge that sleep is a critical part of life. But teens obviously didn't hear about this scientific discovery. On average, Mounds View students get seven and a half hours of sleep when teenagers need nine to function correctly."

They explain the findings that sleep loss impairs cognitive function, causes acne, and disrupts eating patterns—and they explain what happens in the brain during sleep—and conclude, *"It's time for teens to recognize the centrality of sleep to human health."*

Lydia Grimes, who worked on this PSA, says, "It was a good way for me to learn because our group was forced to think about how sleep deprivation affects our own unique situations, rather than focusing on the stereotypical side effects of losing sleep" (personal interview, February 17, 2017).

PBL can also help us develop more inquiry-based strategies for daily lessons, ones that don't merit a whole PBL unit of study.

NCTM's Mathematics Teacher blog ran a series of articles in fall 2016 aimed at helping high school math teachers figure out how to transition to problem-based instruction. They advocated structuring the classroom around students working collaboratively on problems, very similar to what Mary Chin is doing in her discussion-based approach at Arete Preparatory Academy in Arizona (classroom observation, January 10, 2017).

Chin's students work in pods of three to four each day, reviewing homework problems, putting their solutions on whiteboards, then embarking on new problems that introduce challenging new concepts. "The problem gives the 'in' to sort of discover it. Subsequent problems build on it slowly enough that students can say, 'I know what they're talking about.' Sometimes I need to jump in and say, 'Here's what we've learned,'" Chin says.

In one class period, her students were working on this problem from Phillips Exeter Academy's Mathematics 2 curriculum.

> *1. Let E = (2,7) and F = (10,1). On the line through*
> *E and F, there are two points that are 3 units from E.*
> *Find coordinates for both of them.*

Two girls seated together work their way through the problem.

"I did not get [problem] 26-1. I did not know how to do that."

"There are two points that are 3 units from E," her classmate explains, drawing the line in her notebook. "Isn't this something where you do the slope to make the circle?"

Another girl jumps in. *"It said that it had to be 3 units from E. Three up? It could be any direction."*

"I was so confused," the first girl repeats. *"But it says there are two points that are 3 units from E?"*

Chin stops by their table and looks at their work. *"Oh, because it's the line and not a line segment. It's not a clean number,"* she says.

"So basically, it's on the line, in the circle?" the first girl asks. *"From E to F, that's a line? You want to find where it is on the other side. Don't we not know that one either?"*

After a few seconds of thinking, her classmate starts to explain again. *"You want to find the length—you know how we did the Pythagorean theorem? And then find this distance."* She points to the line including E and F. *"Take 3 over 10 and then just multiply by the vector."*

The first girl nods; she gets it now.

"I try to pick problems that are a little more challenging for them to do in class together; that's what's so cool," Chin says.

PBL can also be used to help students review and solidify their learning of new content in a traditional course. University of Illinois professor Gloriana González worked with a geometry teacher at a large midwestern high school to develop a problem-based lesson called the *Circle* problem, which was used during a unit on circles. Like Chin's students, these students had already learned relevant concepts like the Pythagorean theorem and theorems about the geometric mean in right triangles.

On the first day of the PBL lesson, students were placed in small groups, given a diagram of a circle with a few angles labeled and told simply to "find as much information as possible about the segments and the angles in the diagram." On the second day, the teacher led a whole-class discussion of the solutions. One of the benefits of this lesson, the researchers concluded, was that the students were free to define the problem and seek solutions with alternative strategies. "The twenty-two students whose work we analyzed used a total of sixty strategies; thus, on average, each student used about three different strategies to work on the problem" (González and DeJarnette 2013, 588). The students made their own logical connections, learned from their own mistakes, and developed their own ability to think mathematically.

In the past few years, I have used PBL principles to change the way I introduce new concepts and models, especially in economics. Like most econ teachers, I used to simply present and explain each new model to students, then give them time to practice using it. Now I often start by asking my students to reason out each model for themselves. For example, once they have learned the microeconomic model for analyzing a perfectly competitive market (see Figure 5.1), I ask students to list the differences between perfect competition and monopoly (many firms versus one firm, for example), then work with a partner to propose what they think the monopoly graph should look like.

Figure 5.1
PERFECTLY COMPETITIVE MARKET EQUILIBRIUM

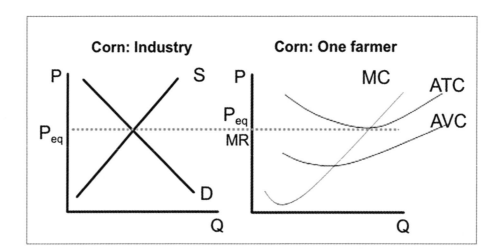

Students try drawing the monopoly graph in all sorts of different ways, but some are quickly able to reason out that because there is only one producer in a monopoly, the graph on the right (one farmer) is basically the monopoly graph, but they need to add a demand curve to represent the consumers. Many are able to come up with something like the graph shown in Figure 5.2 on their own, and those who can't are at least more curious about what monopoly looks like—ready for "telling"—than they would have been. Their peers can explain it to them, and I can fill in the gaps, such as adding the monopolist's marginal revenue curve.

(For readers curious about the graphs, the individual farmer graph in 5.1 shows how marginal costs of production [MC] rise with increased output, which causes increases in average total costs [ATC] and average variable costs [AVC] as well. Marginal revenue [MR] for the individual farmer is a constant price because they can sell as many as they want at the market price, but for a monopolist MR falls as output rises.)

Figure 5.2

FIRST ATTEMPT AT MONOPOLY

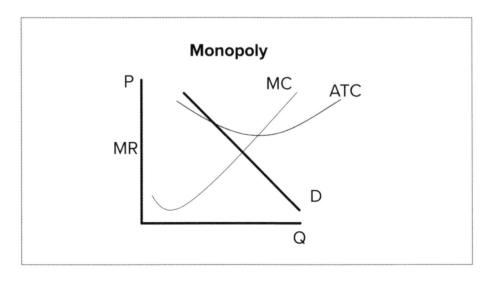

WHAT ARE THE CHALLENGES OF USING PBL?

The research says it is effective; national organizations say it is important. If Problem-Based Learning is so great, why aren't we using it already?

The biggest barrier to PBL is that most American teachers don't know how to do it—we were never taught this way in our own school years—and we are wary. I understand this. I have always thought my students needed me to explain difficult concepts—how could they figure them out otherwise? I also enjoy explaining something and seeing lightbulbs go on; it's one of the pleasures of teaching. Our culture around teaching supports this approach. We are the experts, and our students are the recipients of our knowledge.

There are several problems with this way of thinking. One is that it limits students to learning what we know. I know next to nothing about California's water policy (or riparian rights) or year-round school calendars or the appropriateness of the ALC school model. Why should my knowledge base limit what my students are going to learn? This approach also embraces the old (and discredited) "empty vessel" theory of education. Students don't come to us as empty vessels to be filled with our knowledge. They come with active brains, ready to make connections and reason for themselves. The "expert" culture makes teaching about us, the teachers, and what we know, rather than the students and what they need to learn.

What's interesting about Problem-Based Learning is that it doesn't really diminish our role. Instead, it forces us to change the way we share knowledge and stimulate student thinking. You actually have to know a lot more to be able to teach with PBL. When I first started teaching the monopoly model in economics about ten years ago, I botched it pretty badly. The best I could do (honestly) was draw it on the board and say, "See, it looks like that." (One of my most embarrassing moments was trying to teach this in front of an observing preservice teacher; I broke out in a sweat.)

It took me several years to understand monopoly well enough that I could let the students try to figure it out, look at their work, and be able to ask the kinds of questions that help them create their own understanding. I had to really understand why the marginal revenue curve drops more quickly than the demand curve for a monopolist—because they have to reduce the price to sell more goods—and figure out how to get students to generate that idea. *What will be different with a monopoly? Will they have a supply curve? A demand curve? Can they charge a constant price for each good? What hap-*

pened when Apple lowered the price on its first-generation iPhone? Did they refund the early adopters?

Assigning an open-ended essay, such as the assignment based on the Federal Reserve Essay Contest mentioned earlier, similarly requires a deep understanding of how students write and how they organize their thinking. I've seen many English teachers start by introducing a structure: state the problem, explore causes and effects, offer solutions, use supporting details, explain how to solve the problem. I treat the Federal Reserve Essay like any other PBL assignment. When we started the 2017 topic—*Can the US economy still grow the way it once did?*—I asked students to brainstorm a list of other questions they'd have to answer first. They came up with the following:

> *How did the economy used to grow? When?*
>
> *Why did it stop?*
>
> *How is it growing now? Why?*
>
> *What factors cause it to grow?*

I introduced them to some resources—including an NPR article on worker productivity—and a brief explanation of real GDP (Gross Domestic Product) and per capita real GDP, explained the essay parameters (three pages, double-spaced, MLA style), and set them free. Some students turned in papers that were just one paragraph long. Some failed to identify a problem. Some wrote rigid five-paragraph essays with no supporting evidence. Some wrote in stream of consciousness. Some avoided answering the question.

And my job was to read each essay on its own merits and teach them through feedback (rather than prevention). Libby Fleming's 2016 essay was easy—I just suggested that she delete general statements like "There are lots of solutions" and provide more facts to support her argument. She added PISA rankings and data from a Baltimore research study.

Other essays may require more extensive comments (as many as fifty, in some cases!), depending on where each student is in his or her development. Following are a few examples of comments made on one education essay:

- Don't include so much of your evidence in the intro. Clarify the problem you are trying to solve (low academic performance by American students) and provide evidence of this problem.

- Establish the connection between attention (your solution) and performance. How do we know students will perform better as a result?

- You get to propose only one solution for this paper, so you need to choose.

One way to address our fear and lack of experience is to train teachers better in how to use PBL. It's not as simple as moving from "teacher-directed" to "student-directed"; teachers have to learn how and when to provide support, and how to guide student learning with questions rather than answers. This comes with practice, but it's easier to develop if teachers are encouraged to work with colleagues to develop problem-based lessons, and if they have the time to reflect on and improve the lessons.

Teachers are not the only ones wary of PBL. Another barrier is student and parent resistance. Candice Ridlon (2009) observed this in her two-year study of PBL math in a rural southern school. Just prior to her study, the district had been through a "math war" over the selection of new curriculum. The community, mostly made up of working-class parents, had opposed the adoption of inquiry-based materials, instead fighting for a traditional math textbook, the kind they had used in school. The district was open to her study, though, because school personnel had read previous studies showing that low-income students from disadvantaged backgrounds performed better in problem-centered classrooms. Once the parents saw the changes in student attitude and performance in the study, they began to support PBL.

Student resistance to PBL is mostly a knee-jerk reaction to doing work. If everything else is equal, high school students generally prefer doing less work to doing more work, and PBL is more work. The secret is this: it's a different kind of work, a kind most students later realize they prefer, if they get the opportunity to do it. Viktor Tesarcyzk, another of Ethan Cherin's students, describes UrbanPlan this way: "It was kind of cool, to do it firsthand. It's really not what you learn in the textbooks. You could see all of the terms you read in textbooks and have to memorize, but you're doing it" (personal interview, January 15, 2016).

Another barrier, of course, is high-stakes testing and the perception that the only way to help low-performing students is to keep drilling them on content that they haven't mastered yet. So much of the curriculum we develop is focused on this kind of repetition: defining vocabulary, practicing equations, memorizing details like "Who won the battle at Gettysburg?" Imagine, instead, developing a PBL activity that asked students to determine what General Robert E. Lee could have done differently in order to win at Gettysburg. Think of all the questions the students could generate and all the information they would have to collect in order to come up with a better battle plan. They would have to understand the battle—and war itself—at a deeper level.

One final barrier to using PBL should be mentioned, and that is our misunderstanding of what it means to teach students through open-ended problem solving. According to Ridlon (2009), 95 percent of math teachers say they are aware of NCTM standards for Problem-Based Learning, and 70 percent say they are using this strategy in their classroom, but observations reveal that most classrooms remain pretty traditional. This is not just true for math. Training is key to helping us understand exactly what PBL looks like in action and learn to do it.

TIPS FOR TEACHERS

How do I get started if I have never used Problem-Based Learning?

- If possible, sign up for training or attend a workshop that models PBL. If not, consider buying a prepackaged PBL unit for your first attempt. The unit should include a teacher guide as well as the materials students need and teacher-tested tips for guiding students through the lesson.

- Train students in the process of collaborating, developing their own questions, seeking information, and brainstorming solutions with smaller, day-to-day problems before launching a PBL unit, so the skills and practices will be more familiar.

- Work on developing a short (one- to two-day) PBL unit with your professional learning community, so that multiple teachers can suggest materials and strategies, gather feedback, and refine.

- Remember to focus on the quality of the problem. An effective problem must be complex, ill-structured, and open to multiple solutions, and it must be made relevant to student interests. Many PBL lessons start with a good story, so integrate storytelling techniques here too.

How can I build on my use of PBL to encourage better problem solving and content learning?

- Once you have some practice with effective PBL strategies in daily lessons or one- to two-day units, consider turning one or two weeks of your class into a problem-based investigation. Prepare by gathering a variety of source material, including text, video, diagrams, guest speakers, and other resources.

- Gradually reduce the amount of direct instruction to encourage more student questioning and student ownership of the learning process.

- Ask a colleague to observe your class or videotape yourself, to make sure that whenever possible, you are asking guiding questions rather than providing answers to students.

How will I assess and know if it's effective?

- Use the same assessments you are using now to compare the effectiveness of teaching content through PBL.

- Use a delayed posttest or cumulative test to see whether long-term student retention improves with PBL.

- Survey students to measure engagement and motivation in the course.

- Compare student engagement levels with traditional instruction and PBL by videotaping the class and tabulating voluntary student contributions and student on-task behavior.

6

SIMULATION: IMMERSE STUDENTS IN THOUGHTFUL ROLE PLAYS

The classroom door opens, and teenagers spill in from the hall, colorful scarves flowing, books clutched to chests, a few boys elbowing past to get straight to their desks while girls huddle with friends near the door. Mr. Joel, the teacher, stops them, extending his arm like a friendly traffic cop. "We had a little incident last hour," he tells them. "Just grab a seat back here. . . . What happened is somebody cut their leg—see that little thing sticking out?"

The boys, puzzled, glance at the desks along the wall, and others now turn their heads. One boy walks over as if to investigate, then draws back. The school custodian stands near the desk in question, creating a psychological barrier. "We'll figure something out. I'm sorry," the teacher says.

The twenty-eight students now crowd into the back of the room, accepting that the desks are unusable. A few have found chairs or a ledge to sit on. The girls, all in long skirts, crouch down or sit on the floor. At least it's carpeted. "Are you OK?" the teacher asks them.

"No," one girl quickly responds.

The teacher turns to three boys crowded at a table. "How did you guys even get the seats?" he asks.

"First come, first served!" one answers.

"Well, I don't know if that's fair," says the teacher.

"That's very fair," a boy says.

The teacher turns back to the larger group and starts the day's lesson, a recap of the previous night's reading, then interrupts himself. "I still don't think this is very fair, though," he says, and he scans the faces. He asks the students to think of another way to decide who gets to sit in a chair.

"Get more chairs!" one says.

Others chime in: "I'll bring a chair from home."

"I'm thinking of a number one to ten, and whoever gets it, they'll get my chair."

One girl adds quietly, "Whoever has money . . ."

"Wait, say that again," says the teacher.

"Whoever has money," she says.

The teacher seizes on this idea, and in a moment, he's collecting sealed bids from all the students, some jokingly offering to pay 40 dollars; others offering only friendship; others making genuine bids of 50 cents, 70 cents, even a few dollars. He reads off their names and takes their money and—much to their surprise—reassigns the few chairs to kids who have paid. When they've all settled down again and started to talk seriously about the day's topic, scarcity and resources, he stops again and asks them, "Do you guys think that was actually fair, what we did?"

"That's what we do in real life," one of the girls responds.

"That's true," the teacher says. "What we just did is kind of real life"
(classroom observation, January 26, 2016).

WHAT IS SIMULATION?

Immerse your students in a problem without a clear way to solve it and let them figure out what to do next. While they're puzzling over it, they'll learn problem-solving skills, speaking skills, and collaboration skills along with their terms and theories. Participating in an activity like *Scarce Chairs* is different from reading about or listening to a problem—the students in a simulation experience the frustration of a problem firsthand, creating both relevance and urgency. The question isn't abstract, like, *How should an economy best make use of its resources?* but concrete: *Where am I going to sit today?*

Simulations can be playful and energizing; they can also be intensely serious—a constitutional convention, a witch trial, a climate treaty negotiation. They can be as brief as five minutes or as long as a semester, and they can be live action or virtual, scripted or improvised. Simulation is intensely engaging to students, and the more authentic the situation, the better. Simulation taps into our brain's "seeking system," giving students opportunities for play, firsthand learning, and collaboration, all in a relevant activity. Teenagers in particular love the chance to step outside their real lives, try on different roles, and try out adult problem-solving skills.

Some curriculum writers use the terms *role play* or *serious game* instead of *simulation*—but role plays are only one type of simulation, and simulations are fundamentally different from games that focus on competition or meeting a specific goal. (We'll revisit competition in Chapter 7.) The point is not to win a simulation but to think broadly about options, possibilities, and differing perspectives; the problem presented is messy and the outcome is intentionally ambiguous, similar to Problem-Based Learning. In more extensive simulations, students take on specific character roles to be part of a realistic, clearly defined scenario, like scientists researching the causes of an epidemic or world leaders negotiating the Treaty of Versailles.

Simulation is a way to expand on Problem-Based Learning by immersing students in the "problem." Research has shown that when it's used well—and debriefed effectively, so that students understand and can explain what they have experienced—simulation not only engages and motivates students, but builds enduring factual knowledge and critical-thinking skills.

WHY USE SIMULATION?

Joel Coleman is a young teacher, less than a decade out of high school himself, with a theatrical flair. He smiles constantly, addresses each student warmly by name, and keeps them on task without raising his voice. They call him Mr. Joel, and he treats them with a kind of older-brother-ish devotion, using storytelling techniques to connect them personally to each lesson. He joked with them during *Scarce Chairs* that the money he collected (which he later returned) would go to buying baby supplies—he and his wife were expecting (classroom observation, January 26, 2016).

Coleman uses simulations whenever he can, especially in teaching economics. "It's how I learn the best myself," he explains. "Instead of just being told what it is and how it works . . . just jumping in and doing it." He used *Scarce Chairs* on the second day of class for his regular and college-level economics courses at Ubah Medical Academy, a charter school west of Minneapolis serving primarily Somali American teens. Coleman was pleased with how it went. "Sometimes it takes much longer for them to get to this idea of using money, and sometimes I have to give bigger hints to help them come up with a solution," he says.

Scarce Chairs worked for several reasons. First, the novelty alone nudged the students out of their comfort zone and forced them to pay attention. No one was bored or apathetic in this classroom; you could see the students processing, *What is going on here? What will happen next?* They couldn't not pay attention. The activity also fostered a sense of community. Coleman was "protecting" the students from a "dangerous situation," and he was empowering them to collaborate and think of their own divergent solutions.

Novelty, fun, and connection all trigger dopamine release, and this fostered engagement and drew the students into the lesson. Most important, the activity thrust the students into a situation of "scarcity," and they were forced to think about what that word actually means, beyond just reading it in a textbook. Coleman went on to explain that chairs aren't really what's scarce—it's productive resources that are scarce, and that's why we must choose how to best use them to fulfill our unlimited wants and needs—but they had already internalized that sense of wanting something unattainable.

Coleman started using *Scarce Chairs* during one of his first years of teaching. He couldn't stand watching his students' eyes glaze over while he talked about economics, which he loves but a lot of people find dull. He wanted to grab the students' attention.

"The first day I introduce them to the world of economics is going to be a boring notes day?" he says (personal interview, December 16, 2015). "I needed to do something."

Taking the next step to try an unscripted simulation required some bravery. The first time through, Coleman recalled, he rehearsed his instructions, put on his game face, and waited for the students with apprehension. "I was scared to death trying it. Honestly, there's so much flow with it . . . I didn't get good at it until a year later. . . . There's so much you have to keep focused on and keep cool at the same time."

Coleman's theater background helped him keep a deadpan face and pull it off, even the first time, but there were still challenges. He didn't know at first how to rein in the random student comments, ask the right questions, and help steer students toward a deep understanding of scarcity, choice, and opportunity cost—all critical to making the simulation meaningful. Simulation requires a large degree of letting go, but it also requires an invisible structure, to ensure that learning is actually happening. It is much easier just to keep order and tell students what you want them to know. Watching the chaos unfold as students began talking, laughing, arguing, and moving around was terrifying, he said.

Since then, Coleman has learned to trust in the students and the power of the experience. Every semester, he tries more simulations.

"If it fails, it fails. Fine. You've got to take the risk," he says.

I also tried my first simulation very early in my teaching career; I was lucky to have mine handed to me. Bill Jenkins, my cooperating teacher at Wichita North High School in 1993, shared with me an elaborate role play of a congressional hearing on the US entry into World War I. Every student was assigned a role—one student was prominent socialist Eugene V. Debs, for example; others played people like William Jennings Bryan, J. P. Morgan Jr., Samuel Gompers, and President Woodrow Wilson.

When I started teaching US history in Minnesota a few years later, I decided to pull out his lesson and try it. After months of using mostly lecture, written work, or group projects, I was nervous to see how my group of thirty-five easily distracted sophomores would handle an open-ended task. I gave them one day in the library to research their roles, to try to add a little color and detail to their assigned views on entering the war. Then we held the hearing over two days, listening to twenty individuals testify for and against the US entry into the war.

It started out shakily as the first few students quietly gave their testimony and stepped down, but it didn't take long before the magic started working. The students on the panel started asking challenging questions; the students offering testimony grew more and more emphatic about their positions. Sixteen-year-olds who had known virtually nothing about World War I a week prior (and who cared even less) were suddenly deeply invested in the potential impacts on banks, farmers, and allies. In the debriefing, I asked the class how they felt about this decision-making process. *Who should decide whether or when the United States enters a war? What factors should be considered? Whom should we listen to?* This was the critical moment—the moment when I would see what they had learned.

One girl, Angela, spoke up, and I remember her comments still. She said she'd never thought about the decision to go to war before. "But we need to involve the people," she said. "We need to educate all the people so they can make these decisions for themselves." It was a profound moment. I don't think I could have gotten Angela to that understanding of war powers, the democratic process—or public education—by using lectures, readings, or even a paper. She had to live it.

I've seen the same level of deep understanding emerge from Supreme Court simulations, market simulations, simulations of psych experiments, and many more. In one Supreme Court simulation I used with my US Government class, students were assigned to play the roles of justices and lawyers during the oral arguments of *Safford v. Redding*, a case that considered whether a young girl's right to protection from search and seizure was violated by a strip search at school.

Rather than acting impromptu, the students read from an edited transcript of the case, which I created from the actual transcript. By performing this case as a simulated oral argument, students experienced how the court works, how justices actually interact, and what kinds of questions they raise. In the end, they had to decide the case—in an unscripted deliberation.

In the following segment, students listen as the justices have a surprisingly informal conversation—and see the school district's lawyer try to steer them back to the ruling he wants. Students enjoyed reading the transcript aloud and trying to sound official and stern.

> **Mr. Wright (attorney for the school district):** *We would ask the Court, and it's our position that the Court should lay down a bright line rule. . . . Once you had reason to suspect a student is possessing any contraband that poses a health and safety risk, then searching any place where that contraband may reasonably be found is constitutional, and . . .*

Justice Scalia: Any contraband, like the black marker pencil that— that astounded me. That was contraband in that school, wasn't it, a black marker pencil?

Mr. Wright: Well, for sniffing.

Justice Scalia: Oh, is that what they do?

Mr. Wright: It's a permanent marker.

Justice Scalia: They sniff them?

Mr. Wright: Well, that's the—I mean, I'm a school lawyer. That's what kids do, Your Honor, unfortunately, Your Honor. But . . .

Justice Scalia: Really?

Mr. Wright: But the point is that the rule—the rule, Your Honor—is grounded in the notion that when there's a health and safety risk because these people are charged and tasked with the responsibility to keep these kids safe, they have to have the opportunity to act flexibly, immediately, and effectively when they're dealing with these risks.

Justice Ginsburg: But there has to be—I mean the stark difference between this case and T.L.O., in addition to the intrusiveness of the search, was that in T.L.O., there was a teacher who said: "I caught those girls; they were smoking in the bathroom." Here we have nothing but this girl identifying her classmate. And nothing is done to check her veracity, nothing is done to follow up on it at all. And the search is quite different from the search of a purse that doesn't touch the child's person.

The students were fascinated by the give-and-take of the conversation. *Did they really say that? Do they always interrupt people? Wouldn't it be scary to argue in front of them?* They also liked hearing someone like Justice Ginsburg raise the issue of relying on one student's tip to go search another student. *Isn't that just a rumor?* In some classes, the students decided in favor of the young girl, Savannah Redding, but others sided with the school. By listening to the arguments and making their own, they began to understand the school's concern—and the court's concern—about letting schools address potentially risky drug situations.

In economics class, I use a very different kind of simulation that relies on students' impromptu behavior, rather than a script. A market simulation, like the *Market in Cocoa* (*High School Economics* 2014), helps students experience supply and demand in a way that dry economics graphs never convey. Some students are assigned to be buyers of cocoa beans and are given cards that tell them how much they're willing to pay but that they would prefer to pay less. Others are given seller cards and told the price they need in order to break even but are encouraged to sell for more. Then, for about fifteen minutes, the students negotiate on their own and try to make deals. An equilibrium price emerges, almost like magic.

"When we did that in macro, it gave this fantastic sense of 'Oh, look at that, it's supply and demand,'" Jacob Weightman says. "I think one of the things I really appreciated about that is it was so clear what it illustrated. It worked really well. It's hard to model a lot of things in economics, but when we set up the market this way, it shows exactly what the demand curve and supply curve look like" (personal interview, October 26, 2016).

Simulations can also help students experience something they would not be able to see for themselves, like electrons moving in a container or what happens at the chemical level in a neuron. Kelly Gallagher (personal interview, October 13, 2016), who teaches chemistry and anatomy/physiology in Linden, New Jersey, uses online PhET (Physics Education Technology; https://phet.colorado.edu/) simulations for both of these concepts. Students, acting as researchers with high-tech equipment, can manipulate the temperature or size of a container and see how it impacts the electrons. "It's usually hard because they're trying to imagine electrons," she says. Same with neurons—the simulation of ions moving across barriers makes it a lot more engaging. "I had to painstakingly memorize from a dry old textbook when I learned it," she says.

Eric Friberg and Jen Nippert also use a PhET simulation when they teach about natural selection. In this one, wolves are hunting white bunnies and brown bunnies in a desert, and students can observe that the white bunnies are easier to catch, because they're easier to see. The students act as scientists collecting data, and over time—which is compressed in the computer simulation—the white bunny population diminishes, while the brown bunny population, which starts with one mutation, endures and begins to grow. "The kids are able to see something that happens over a long period of time in a short period of time," Friberg says. "It's at a very relatable level."

In one of Friberg's classes, Patricia Taylor and Margaret Roberts, two of his students, saw the impact as soon as they added wolves to the desert ecosystem (classroom observation, March 15, 2017). One click, and the white bunny population was in decline.

"All the white rabbits can't even blend in," Margaret says.

"What's the number of brown rabbits?" Patricia says. "About fifteen?"

"And the white rabbits are forty-five, maybe forty-four."

They let the simulation run for three more generations, and Margaret announces, "All the white ones are dying!"

"Because the brown ones are camouflaged. . . . And then the next group of wolves comes."

"Whoa," Margaret says. "The white population is so far down. I'm going to zoom in and see how accurate we can get on this. Only three left."

"And how many brown?" asks Patricia. "Thirteen?"

"The brown variation allowed the bunnies to blend in to their environment as a form of protection," Margaret concludes later, as they write up their results. "It definitely has something to do with, How useful is the trait to the environment?"

Like my students experiencing the real-life negotiations of buyers and sellers, they were able to learn by doing—rather than just listening.

In 2000, researchers from Harvard and Arizona State University developed an extensive online simulation called *River City*, with support from the National Science Foundation, to provide insight into the effectiveness of simulations (http://rivercity.activeworlds.com/). In *River City*, which was designed for middle school science, students time-traveled back to a nineteenth-century industrial city to help the mayor figure out why residents had fallen ill. The students interviewed virtual residents, examined historical photographs, heard mosquitoes buzzing and people coughing, and used tools like a virtual microscope to examine water samples. *River City* was used with thousands of students and studied extensively in controlled trials. The students who learned with this simulation showed more motivation for science learning, improved self-efficacy, improved inquiry skills, better behavior in class, and no loss of content knowledge.

According to a report by the National Research Council, "in the *River City* classrooms, students and teachers were highly engaged, student attendance improved, and disruptive behavior dropped during the three-week implementation period. In interviews, students who played *River City* reported that they were motivated by the ability to conduct inquiry, along with the ability to use virtual tools, such as bug catchers and microscopes to aid in their investigations" (Honey and Hilton 2011, 38).

I've observed similar results with simulations in my classroom. During simulations, cell phones disappear, students become energized and focused, and their effort looks more like play than work. It's not surprising—what they are doing is fun. And as indicated earlier, when students are having fun, their brains are flooded with dopamine, which increases their motivation, focus, and attention. Students say they like the discovery process and the *aha* moment during the debriefing, when the concept suddenly becomes clear.

"It's good because it allows people to almost discover for themselves what you're teaching them," says Sola Olateju, a former student who was always one of the first to volunteer for any simulation. "When you explain the concept, they're like 'Oh, that makes so much sense. I just participated in that.' You don't even recall how you know it so well because it's just natural to you" (personal interview, October 26, 2016).

HOW DO YOU INCLUDE SIMULATION IN YOUR INSTRUCTION?

Teaching through simulation is an entirely different skill from preparing PowerPoint slides and assigning worksheets, or even constructing self-directed lessons or group work. If teaching is an art, simulation is the most sophisticated level of performance.

The first thing I learned from using simulations was not to oversell them. If you tell high school students, "Today is going to be fun" or "We're going to do something really cool today," they will do their best not to be impressed. They are teenagers, after all. When I'm starting a simulation, I introduce the situation, explain the students' roles, and appeal to their imaginations, but I don't promise anything. It's easier to give them a pleasant surprise than to live up to high expectations.

Second, simulations work only if they involve a realistic challenge or underlying conflict. The World War I simulation worked because it engaged students in a real issue: *When should the United States involve itself in conflicts between other nations? River City* worked because students had a pressing question to answer: *What is making people sick?* Like discussions where everyone agrees, simulations that are too simplistic or easy to resolve don't stimulate long-term learning.

Third, simulations must let students be creative and have fun. They can't be too structured or constrained. If the situation is "real," then once it is set in motion, most student behavior within the simulation will reflect real life. The key for the teacher is to know how to react, and that takes practice.

I have used one of my favorite simulations, *The Circular Flows of Econoland*, dozens of times in my regular and AP Macroeconomics classes, as well as in workshops for new economics teachers, and every time, I learn from it (*High School Economics* 2014). *Econoland* fits in the first week of the semester, and it is the students' first exposure to models of how households and firms interact in an economy. It's relatively easy to set up but nearly impossible to control. But if you understand economic principles well, you can integrate almost every student behavior into the learning experience.

When students come to class on *Econoland* day, they take their seats, and I hand them either a stack of play $100 bills or a handful of small items, like screws, balsa wood, or googly eyes. They leave their notebooks in backpacks and start talking to each other, uncertain what to expect and a little nervous. I explain that if they have money, they will be considered "firms." We talk for a few minutes about what firms are—Starbucks, Ford, Apple, 3M—and where that money came from. Do they have investors? A bank loan? Grandma? We talk a little about how entrepreneurs actually get startup cash (like *Shark Tank*), which gets them thinking from a firm's perspective.

Then I explain that the rest of the class—those who can't keep their hands off the googly eyes, balsa, and screws—are "households." The googly eyes represent labor; the balsa, land; the screws, capital. Again, we talk for a few minutes, this time about why households own the resources, such as their own labor and ideas as well as land.

Then I explain what's going to happen: business firms are going to produce colored puffballs, which represent everything a consumer could want—a two-story house in a pleasant neighborhood, a sports car or minivan (whichever you prefer), a vacation in Florida. The firms need to buy resources if they are going to produce puffballs, just like coffee shops need to buy beans, water, coffeepots, workers, and so on, before they can prepare coffee to sell to customers. In class, firms will need to buy the screws, googly eyes, and balsa from the households. Once a firm has one of each resource, they can "make" a puffball by bringing the resources to me.

"Consumers want puffballs," I emphasize, "and firms want profits."

There are usually a few questions, such as

> *Which one is people?*
>
> *Where do we get resources?*
>
> *How many kinds of resources are there?*
>
> *What do I want—money or puffballs?*

After answering the questions, I open the market, and the firms begin to buy resources, making puffballs as fast as they can to sell to consumers. The simulation may sound complicated, but to teenagers it is as natural as breathing. Their goals are not difficult to remember—they either want stuff or money, just like in real life. Their conversations sound like a chaotic street market.

"I have two puffballs . . ."
"$200!"
"OK, wait, I have—"
"One for $100."
"I literally don't even know how much I have."
"I'm a businessman."
"These are mine. I bought these!"
"I bought two eyeballs for $100—and sold them for $200!"
"Does anybody want eyes or wood?"
"There's not enough resources; we're out of screws."

Often, the students playing firms try to lowball the households, demanding two resources for $100. The households hold out for $100 apiece or more, sometimes forming cartels to hoard the resources. There's shouting, arguing, side deals ("I'll give you a real dollar if you sell to me"), frustration, and eventually, a mostly working market. Most of the resources are transformed into puffballs, and some households accumulate a big pile of them. Some of the firms end up with more money than they started with, and others take losses. In all, it takes about twenty-five minutes.

The activity, published by the Council for Economic Education years ago, is designed to teach students the Circular Flow Diagram, a complicated concept that shows how households and firms operate in both resource and product markets. In the process, students also learn a little about *entrepreneurship, scarcity, competition, costs, price, profit, producers, consumers, supply, demand, recession,* and *income inequality*. They don't even notice as these ideas slip into their minds and become part of their vocabulary.

One freshman, brand-new to economics, explains how he successfully (and instinctively) earned profits: "So what I did was, sometimes resources were scarcer on one side of the room, so I went to the other side where they weren't, and I bought them for less. Usually, I could get multiple for $100."

Will Tjernlund, a former student, said he realized while playing *Econoland* that this was what he wanted to do with his life. "I thought, 'If I can get good at this game, I will be able to negotiate and strategize my way to the top of the business ladder.' I had never had that feeling in class before. I always assumed I would not be using anything I learned in school in the real world, but this activity felt different" (personal interview, December 6, 2016).

Students become deeply engaged in *Econoland*, but they also try to outsmart or even undermine the game, which can frustrate teachers. I used to try to rein in this behavior, but as I've gained experience and become more comfortable with the simulation, I've come to see these behaviors as teachable moments.

For example:

- The firms often try to cut costs and rip off their classmates who are playing households, just for fun. Later, they find out the hard way that if households' income goes down, no one can afford to buy the products, and they don't earn much money. It's a perfect segue into talking about the causes of recession.

- Sometimes households will join together to control a resource and raise prices. Students see that collusion benefits the colluders, but it ripples out and hurts the other households, who lose income and can't afford the more expensive puffballs. A good argument for anti-trust laws.

- Some students are blasé about business and don't try to buy low or sell high. They want to sit back and watch. Like poor business managers or households without personal finance skills, they quickly go bankrupt—a good reminder that initiative and human capital can impact your future income and lifestyle, though they are not the only factors.

- Some students hold out too long for a higher (or lower) price and are left holding unused resources—extra googly eyes, screws, and wood—at the end. These idle resources simulate unemployed workers, abandoned factories, and unplanted fields. Without them, not enough will be produced, and the *Econoland* economy will shrink.

Every simulation works slightly differently, especially in terms of how students learn. In the World War I hearing and the Supreme Court argument, the students had to immerse themselves in specific, assigned roles, and the learning occurred collaboratively as they listened, argued, and processed the various reasons for and against going to war—like pieces of a large jigsaw puzzle fitting together. In *Econoland*, as with *Scarce Chairs* and the *Market in Cocoa*, the roles are more generic, and the learning comes simply from acting like any consumer or producer. The students follow the rules and their natural instincts—try to get a chair, try to earn money, try to get more stuff—and suddenly they understand how millions of these interactions every day are what creates the national economy. In *River City* and the PhET bunny simulation, the students learn through inquiry. They act as researchers, generating their own hypotheses, conducting firsthand research, and writing up their own conclusions.

Many of the simulations we use in social studies classrooms could also be adapted for English classrooms. Mock trials, for example, give students the opportunity to write witness statements, cross-examine testimony, and practice public speaking. Students reading nonfiction texts about current issues, such as trade policy, can use their sources to create a simulated congressional hearing on a proposed policy, such as President Trump's proposed tariff on imports from Mexico.

The engagement and motivational power of these activities is subtle. Students are drawn in by the roles, by the problems posed, by the opportunity to interact with their peers or technology and have a fun experience. An effective simulation creates a shared understanding that a teacher can refer to over and over during the semester, as we examine in turn each of the issues that came up.

There is one more step, though—a critical step for any teacher using simulations: the debriefing. Experts who have studied simulation say that without effective debriefing, these activities are reduced to simple games—fun and engaging perhaps, but not very educational. David Crookall, an international expert in classroom simulation and gaming, says debriefing is so critical that "it is better not to run a simulation/game if you are not going to debrief it properly" (Crookall 2014, 422). Debriefing doesn't have to be complicated. It's not so different from two teachers meeting at lunch, talking about a difficult class and processing their experience. But because engagement in a simulation can be so strong and emotional, it's critical to help students step back and reflect on what they learned. Students can become so involved in a simulation—for example, getting angry because they ended up bankrupt—that it can overshadow the intended learning.

In *Econoland*, the debriefing gets students to think through what they did, why they did it, and how it impacted other people. I always ask the students who managed to accumulate the most puffballs or cash what they did.

"Well, I got a puffball from someone for $100," a household explains. "And I got a couple people to give me $200 for one piece of land."

I ask the class to consider, "If a business paid $200 for a piece of land and $200 for a screw and $200 for an eyeball, it would cost $600 to make a puffball, right? And the household paid $100 for a puffball. So he managed to get the businesses to pay him a lot for wages but not pay a lot for products."

We trace that on a Circular Flow Diagram on the board, seeing how the flow of money would help the consumer but cause the business to possibly go bankrupt.

A student in the business role explains that he managed to do just the opposite. "Someone sold me wood cheap. I also sold my puffballs for, like, $400 each."

I'll also pick out one household who didn't get any puffballs and ask, "Why not? What happened?" When they explain what happened—maybe they sold too quickly, without realizing the value of their resources—we talk about how that happens to people in the real world, too. People who aren't educated or savvy, who don't realize the value of their skills and abilities, or who face discrimination, can get taken advantage of.

In an online reflection afterward, I ask the students five questions, including, "What did you learn from the simulation?" and "What do you wish you had known before the simulation that you know now?" Their responses vary from practical (how to make more money) to philosophical. (See more student reflections in Appendix B, Chapter 6, Sample 1, available online at sten.pub/beatboredom.) Following are a few examples:

> *I wish I knew how much I could spend and how much I needed to sell products for in order to make a profit. I ended up with exactly what I started with, and figured out that the product had to be sold for more than $300 in order to make up for the cost of the resources that I bought for $100 each.*

> *I learned how the system works and how the flow of money happens, how the resources I put in get back to me in a different way.*

> *Even when all of the goods are evenly distributed at the start, in the end it's impossible for everybody to get everything they want.*

The simulation is where the action happens, but the debriefing and reflection is where students learn to piece together what it means, why it's important, and how it fits in the context of their greater understanding.

WHAT ARE THE CHALLENGES OF USING SIMULATION?

Despite the fun of running simulations—and the many advantages of simulation as a learning tool—many K–12 teachers use them rarely, if ever. The reasons are easy to understand. Simulations take time; they require a leap of faith (to cede control in the classroom); they can be complicated to plan; and there are few opportunities for teacher training, since the majority of professional development spending is focused on testing and technology.

TIME

Perhaps the biggest factor discouraging teachers from using classroom simulations is the time they steal away from other methods of instruction. High-stakes testing and state-mandated content objectives have convinced us that we need to spend every second listing and defining terms, then practicing over and over again on multiple-choice questions, just to get through it all. Lecture may not be effective, but it is certainly quick. It feels like a risk to give up even twenty minutes of explaining for twenty minutes of experiencing. According to Honey and Hilton (2011), in the National Research Council report mentioned earlier, science curriculum coordinators in three large urban districts "refused to allow teachers to use *River City* because an emphasis on science inquiry might interfere with students doing well on content-oriented, high-stakes tests" (63).

It's true: We never have enough time in our classrooms to do all the work that feels urgent, but we're not actually efficient if we're using strategies that don't build retention and long-term understanding. It's also tragic if we give up teaching inquiry to load students with lists of facts instead. One simulation can teach a variety of terms and concepts, as well as critical-thinking, communication, and collaboration skills—and teach them in a way that students won't soon forget. Think about how many terms were introduced in *Econoland*, and in a subtle way that didn't make it feel like "learning."

CLASSROOM MANAGEMENT

For many teachers, especially new teachers without much classroom management experience, the easiest way to deal with students is to keep them quiet in their assigned seats. Doug Lemov, author of *Teach Like a Champion*, advocates requiring the SLANT behaviors: sit up, listen, ask and answer questions, nod your head, track the speaker (Lemov 2010). This might be more rigid than many teachers enforce, but it is not different from what many want. If students are seated in a carefully orchestrated setting, eyes on the teacher and notebooks open, at least it looks like they're learning, even if most of the information will be quickly forgotten. Letting go of that structure is viscerally terrifying, and letting the students get up, walk around, and interact seems like a dicey proposition. *What if they get off task? What if they won't sit back down?* Although simulations have proven to be more effective than traditional lecture with struggling, unfocused students, they are often reserved for use with high-achieving students, because it's easier to trust that they will stay "under control."

The management piece is probably the most intimidating. The shorter and more specific the simulation, the easier it is to keep the classroom feeling under control. Teachers can try five-minute simulations (like *Scarce Chairs*) and build trust with students that participation will be fun and engaging.

PLANNING

There's no question that creating a simulation from scratch takes much longer than planning a lecture or written assignment. Even if the simulation is published and thoroughly explained, like *Econoland* or *River City*, the teacher still has to read and make sense of the instructions, acquire and organize all the supplies, and set up the simulation. And when the first hour is over, you have to quickly put the supplies back in order to be ready for the second hour (or have a second set). It's not easy, especially if you have hall duty or students lined up to ask questions. The planning alone can seem overwhelming—and keeps many teachers from trying simulations.

Planning, although significantly challenging, can be done a little at a time. There are hundreds of prepackaged, tested simulations available online, many of them for free, and teachers can work together in professional learning communities to implement just one simulation in a semester. Experts in many fields are working on developing more simulations, especially in the virtual or "augmented reality" realm, for students in K–12 classrooms. In addition to *River City*, the same NRC report noted other sophisticated science simulations, including the PhET simulations, Physlets, *WolfQuest,* SURGE, Weatherlings, and Whyville (Honey and Hilton 2011). Social studies teachers have access to simulations like mock trials, mock congresses, market simulations, behavioral economics simulations, games like *Chair the Fed* or *Fiscal Ship*, historical reenactments, and sociology simulations, such as STARPOWER.

In psych, I have used simulations to show students what it's like to experience learned helplessness, what it's like to be ostracized, how hearing loss impacts what you hear and understand, how visualizing things improves memory, and how classical conditioning works, to name a few. These are mostly five-to-ten-minute simulations that let students have a memorable shared experience, then debrief and discuss how it illustrates psychological theory.

TRAINING

Even if teachers have the time, the management skills, and the initiative to adopt classroom simulations, they may resist doing so because of a lack of training. Most professional-development dollars today are spent on Common Core State Standards, testing prep, and basic technology training. Teachers who are using simulations need to know how to select, prepare, introduce, administer, assess, and debrief the activities—and they need to carefully avoid turning them into random events, with no clear tie to curricular objectives. Researchers who have studied simulations agree that the best strategy for training teachers is to give them the chance to participate in a simulation. If that isn't possible, they should at least be able to watch someone else conduct one before trying it themselves. I may never have tried a simulation if I hadn't watched Bill Jenkins at North High—or participated in *Econoland* at a Minnesota Council on Economic Education workshop. I remember playing *Econoland* (the professor let us produce Rolo candies instead of puffballs) and becoming very competitive. Unlike my students, I knew what to do—buy resources cheap, sell Rolos at a high price—but that didn't make me good at doing it.

Once you've been a participant, you understand every part of the experience—the questions students will have, the emotions they'll experience, the adrenaline rush of participation, the critical importance of debriefing—and you understand why it is so motivating to students.

Joel Coleman, who started out with *Scarce Chairs*, now uses simulations for all sorts of lessons. His students, many of them first-generation Americans, have role-played scenarios as complex as the Treaty of Versailles negotiations and the Potsdam Conference. Sometimes it takes three to four hours to plan one lesson, and it may not work perfectly. But watching disengaged students perk up and get involved is worth it. Passive learning might be easy, but it doesn't build the skills students need later.

"I try to get out of the way whenever I can and let them take control of their learning," he said. "It's such an important skill for college and for life—just give them a really cool thing to get interested in and let them run with it."

TIPS FOR TEACHERS

How do I get started if I have never used a simulation?

- Training is key to building skills and confidence; if attending a training is not possible, try to at least participate in or watch a simulation before trying it with students. Some teachers post videos of their simulations on YouTube, and frequently a few sessions at professional conferences will involve simulations.

- Rather than writing your own simulations, use prebuilt simulations that come with a teacher's guide and debriefing questions. Organizations like the National Research Council, the Council for Economic Education, and the National Council for Social Studies can provide links to quality simulations; you can also access them through teacher networks (like Twitter) and conferences.

- Start small. Use a five-to-ten-minute simulation before taking on a full-day or multiday simulation, to give yourself practice and help your students develop the skills to participate appropriately.

- Be patient. A simulation might not work the first time. Take copious notes on what you'd do differently, and ask students for their feedback during the debriefing. Students often have valuable insight into what went wrong or how it might work better.

How can I build on my use of simulation to encourage deeper understanding and content learning?

- Think about the debriefing questions and what you want students to say or conclude. If student response does not indicate the understanding or critical thinking you want, analyze what is missing and what kinds of questions you could ask to encourage deeper reflection.

- Once you are comfortable running simulations, expand to more complex scenarios that require students to play specialized roles.

- Ask students to help you develop a simulation, based on a topic you are studying in class. Students can identify key roles and questions and help develop the scenario.

How will I assess and know if it's effective?

- Use the same assessments you are using now to compare the effectiveness of teaching content through simulation.

- Debrief, debrief, debrief. Ask questions during the debriefing to help students build understanding and to help you gauge student understanding. Use exit slips or online formative quizzes (like Kahoot or Socrative, both free web-based quiz programs) to collect insights from all students, rather than just outspoken students.

- Ask students to write a brief reflection after a simulation, answering questions specific to their role, to the experience, and to the learning objectives. I ask my *Econoland* students to explain how their role (household or firm) is involved in the circular flow, what they learned, what they wish they had known beforehand, and what remaining questions they have. Some teachers using more complex simulations (like the World War I hearing) require students to write position statements or character profiles before the actual simulation.

- Use surveys to measure student understanding of the purposes of the simulation and whether it met your intended goals.

7

COMPETITION: GIVE STUDENTS A CHANCE TO PROVE THEMSELVES

It's 6:30 a.m. and dark outside. It won't be light out for more than an hour. A small cadre of students are huddled around a table, ready to slap their hands down on a make-believe buzzer, seeing who can answer economics acronym questions the fastest.

"What do the 3 Ms in 3M—"

Bam. "Minnesota Mining and Manufacturing."

"What are the BRICS countries?"

Bam. "Brazil, Russia, India, China . . . and South Africa?"

"What countries are the PIIGS?"

The students confer. "Portugal?"

"Is it Italy? Ireland?"

"Germany . . . or Greece?"

"Spain."

For three of his four high school years, Jacob Weightman was part of this early-rising group. Some days, he spent six hours just preparing for Economics Challenge competitions—learning acronyms, initialisms, data, and dates as well as difficult theoretical concepts (personal interview, October 26, 2016).

In classes, Jacob admits, he sometimes did just enough to earn an A-. But for Econ Challenge, there was no limit to his effort. After competing in the regular (non-AP) division sophomore year, Jacob wanted to see if he could make the AP team as a junior.

It was a long shot—he hadn't taken AP Micro or AP Macro yet.

"I saw it as sort of a chance to take things as far as I could, in terms of pushing the limits of what I thought I could do," he said. "After qualifying for the team—just barely—I found it really exciting and really engaging to see how far I could push it even beyond that, to see how I stacked up in the metro area . . . in the state of Minnesota . . . at the national level."

When he started out, Jacob just wanted to prove himself. But over time, he also found himself fascinated by the subject. He spent hours googling economic concepts, following one link to the next, trying to piece together obscure theories into a conceptual whole.

"A lot of what I did was digging for deeper understanding of concepts, like the Snackwell effect, bounded rationality, Ricardian equivalence. . . . Within economics, I think a lot of the fun stuff is those smaller theories that are narrower in scope—looking at what might be surprising behavior in certain situations and why it makes sense."

Jacob's team of four—one of hundreds of teams competing nationwide—won the Econ Challenge national championship in New York City that year.

"It ended up honing my skills in a way that couldn't have happened without that competitive format."

WHAT IS COMPETITION?

Competition is pervasive in American society. Athletes compete at Olympic, professional, college, high school, and community levels. High school students compete for admission to college. Aspiring chefs compete on *Iron Chef*. Candidates compete to win elections. And businesses, such as airlines, auto manufacturers, and tech companies, all compete for our precious dollars.

Academic competitions harness this same energy—the innate desire to excel at or achieve something—and we can use it to motivate students to deeper learning.

Competition is not without controversy. For decades, educators have debated the merits of competition in the classroom. In 1986, Alfie Kohn's *No Contest* (1986) was published, making a strong case against any use of competition in schools. Kohn said competition makes children anxious, interferes with concentration, and prevents collaborative learning. Researchers in the 1970s had found that monetary rewards, prizes, deadlines, and "surveillance" undermine students' intrinsic motivation. At the same time Kohn was criticizing competition, other educators were calling for more academic competition, so that students would be recognized for more than just their athletic accomplishments. Charles Duke (1988), a professor of English education at Utah State, argued that teachers should use the power of competition to excite students about learning, the same way coaches instill passion in their players.

Since then, we have learned that the kind of competition matters—as does the kind of coaching—when we look at the impact on kids.

What kind of competition, then, is useful? We all remember some form of competition from our school days. Spelling bees were the most popular in my childhood. We also competed to see who could read the most books—for our teachers during the school year, and for the local library in the summer. In high school, I competed on the speech team and math team. Each of these competitions had some value, in that they motivated me to work a little harder than I might have otherwise, but speech team was the most meaningful to me for several reasons:

- Speech team focused on meaningful tasks. Nothing against spelling bees, but mastering our archaic spelling system isn't as critical as learning to research current events or speak in public.

- Speech team encouraged collaboration. One year, I rehearsed with a partner to develop a "dramatic duo." Another year, I studied and discussed news events with teammates to prepare for "extemp" (extemporaneous speaking). Speech team was never a solo activity, unlike most of my schoolwork. I had to learn how to work with others, and I met people outside my usual friend group.

- Speech team raised the bar for my personal expectations. I thought I was pretty good at acting, until I saw other pairs in the dramatic duo category, like one duo who performed a scene from *Rosen-*

crantz and Guildenstern Are Dead. They were so professional that I vividly remember it thirty years later. My partner and I really had to step up our game.

- Speech team motivated me to do work I wouldn't have done otherwise. Extemp was terrifying, but my team needed another person in that category, and the coach recruited me. In 1983, I had to prepare by reading about the Sandinistas, the civil war in El Salvador, the attack on the US Marines in Lebanon. I had to make myself care about faraway people and places—topics not that interesting to my suburban sixteen-year-old self—because I didn't want to embarrass myself at a meet. The more I read, the more I found myself caring, and the more it opened my eyes to world affairs.

Since the 1980s, academic competitions have expanded and grown far more sophisticated. The best competitions today involve leadership, teamwork, strategy, and purposeful activities that require deep critical thinking. Many are essentially simulations, but with a defined goal. Competitions today engage students in solving problems, managing hypothetical businesses, building robots, making national security decisions, and conducting independent scientific research—to name just a few—and they are very effective at sparking students' interest and motivation.

They also build teamwork, just like baseball and basketball do. Mike Lampert has taken students to nine different national science competitions, and he said his teams "become sort of family. . . . You spend so much time eating pizza; we talk about everything" (personal interview, June 16, 2016). These competitions aren't about individual glory or defeat but about collaboration and purpose.

"Today you don't have a Renaissance man, you don't have one person able to do everything," says Lampert. "People who may not be really talented in the math area may be very talented in the marketing area. . . . You get this group of kids together, and you build off everybody's talents, and it's really rewarding as a coach to see that come together."

In some years, I have taken a few of the same students to as many as five state and national economics competitions, and we get to know each other's stories, quirks, food preferences, insecurities, and ambitions. While we eat together and take walks to touristy sites, they ask questions: "I think I want to study econ. What jobs are there?" "Why did you become a teacher? I'm wondering whether I would like it." "I thought I wanted to go to Harvard, but it's too intense. Where could I go that would be really good but where it's more collaborative?" And of course, inside jokes develop. "Bounded rationality"—an economic term explaining why people don't always make the most logical choice—became shorthand in our team for explaining anything stupid that happens, like losing a room key or not finishing homework.

Many Econ Club kids stay in touch long after they graduate and become friends—with me, with each other, and also with students they meet from other schools.

WHY USE COMPETITION?

"I think finding a purpose in what you do is really important. Even on a vacation, when you are just wandering around, it's not as much fun. But when you reach a peak or see the sunrise there, it gives you a purpose," says Abraham Chen of the 2015 Econ Challenge championship team (personal interview, December 28, 2016).

The National Economics Challenge, or Econ Challenge, is a program of the Council for Economic Education (http://councilforeconed.org/national-economics-challenge) and one of several competitive activities I coach.

If I had read Kohn's work about the potential drawbacks first, I might never have tried competition as a teaching strategy. No one wants to cause their students stress and anxiety, and no one wants any student to feel like a "loser." I think about Maddy's "Defining Moment" essay (see Chapter 3, Sample 2 in the appendix); just one overzealous coach, and it ruined her love of basketball.

But having used competition and seen how it can motivate students like Abraham, it would be very hard to ever give it up. Competition creates a unique energy. Students meet early in the morning, after school, on weekends, or all summer long to prepare for competitions. They e-mail me in the middle of the night when they find new review questions or have new ideas or problems they cannot resolve. (Of course, I don't see the message until morning.) Last year, some of my JA Company Program (created by Junior Achievement USA) students were Skyping regularly with their business volunteer at all hours while he traveled to India and China for his work. With competition, learning is never confined to the school day. (The JA Company Program is explained in Chapter 8—it's an authentic task as well as a competition.)

During competitive activities, whether it's basketball, baseball, or Econ Challenge, adrenaline floods the body, giving us energy and focus. We find it easy to wake up earlier and stay up later. Competition transforms teacher into coach and changes the nature of learning. Rather than asking, *Why do we need to know this?* students involved in competition become highly attuned to their own goals and deficits. Like Jacob, they start to ask, *What more do I need to know? Do I know enough?* One of my students a few years ago, a sophomore girl studying for the regular division of Econ Challenge, recorded herself reading Quiz Bowl questions with delayed answers and listened to this as a podcast while she was running. Needless to say, she was amazing at the competition—she buzzed in first and answered nearly every question correctly.

Kohn expresses concern that competition hurts intrinsic motivation, but I have seen students' fixation on external motivations—like grades—become less important in a competitive setting. The students are completely in the moment, in what Mihaly Csikszentmihalyi (2009) calls "flow," which is why the learning experience is so profound.

One of my favorite competitions is Junior Achievement's Titan competition (http://titan.ja.org/); almost every student at my high school participates, most of them during freshman year, and not for a grade. Titan is an online futuristic simulation, set in 2035. Each team of two to four students is running a business making "Holo-Generators"—think 3-D DVR players—and they are all competing in the same industry. (For the purpose of competition, the industry is divided into segments, so six to eight teams compete in each segment.)

In each business quarter, which is timed by the program, students must make six strategic decisions: they control product price and output level, as well as how much of their budget to dedicate to four areas—marketing, research and development, capital investment, and charitable giving. If a team makes the right decisions, profits will soar, their firm will grow and their performance index will rise, putting them above their competitors. Make the wrong decisions, and they could end up bankrupt. These are not easy decisions to make, because performance depends on what other teams do, just like real-world business competition. If another team undercuts your price or develops a new feature before you do, your firm will hit the skids.

Listening to students involved in this competition is like listening to a business strategy session—or participating in one of Harvard Business School's simulations.

Yuha Yoo, Do-Yun Park, and Collin Frink are working as a team, competing against five other teams in their segment of the industry. They're in second place (classroom observation, December 20, 2016).

Yuha: *We have to increase market share.*

Do-Yun: *Would investment increase it?*

Yuha: *We aren't producing enough.*

Collin: *How is Smell-o-vision coming?*

Do-Yun: *I would do more . . .*

Suddenly, the quarter is closed. The simulator reveals that they have slipped to third place. They want to know what happened.

Do-Yun (looks around): *Who is Group Six?*

Yuha: *We have the second-highest market share. We have the highest sales, too.*

Do-Yun: *What did they do? Our market share is higher than theirs! Should we drop the price to 50? . . . R&D, let's keep it at 500.*

A few minutes later, after the next quarter closes, they drop to fourth place.

Do-Yun (looks at the company report and concludes grimly): *We're not producing enough compared to our marketing.*

I've watched students compete in this simulation in dozens of different settings, from a global competition hosted at the University of Delaware in 2012—my students competed against kids from Russia, Poland, Canada, and China, and placed second to one of the Chinese teams—to an in-class competition at Humboldt High School on the West Side of St. Paul, where 90 percent of the kids are on the free lunch program. Every time, I've seen the same thing: students deeply engaged in making business strategy decisions and learning (without even thinking about it) how to discuss *R&D, marketing, factory capacity,* and the benefit of producing at *minimum average total cost.* They are learning key course concepts in business and economics in a way that's far more memorable than listening to a lecture or reading a textbook.

One of the sophomore boys I met at Humboldt explained to me that his team was trying to keep factory utilization at 80 percent. They were debating how much to put toward charitable contributions. He was advocating for more giving in order to build the firm's reputation.

"People will say, 'Have you seen them? They are amazing, giving back to the community,'" he explains. He adds, "Man, I'm loving this. We've got to stay in first place. I fear we're getting too risky."

Later, when his team has slipped to third, he says, "It's fun, but it's stressful and it's scary. . . . Business management is way harder than we thought it was in the first place."

Competition can open a new world to students, taking them outside the confines of their own high school and its social and academic norms. Melissa Maxcy Wade, the director of forensics at Emory, founded the Urban Debate League (urbandebate.org) in 1985 because she believed in the power of competitive debate to nurture disadvantaged children's potential and help level the playing field for college readiness. The kids who disrupt class and get kicked out because they don't buy into the system are "enfranchised by debate," she says. "Instead of being bad, they walk around saying: 'Wow, I just beat Elite Academy. Look at me!'" (Ruenzel 2002, 24–30).

Steve Jents coaches in the Urban Debate League for Central High School in St. Paul, and he loves seeing that transformation (personal interview, December 15, 2016). "I have a kid that's a smartass that has a 12 percent in my class because he never does anything," says Jents, "but he's a quick wit and he likes being argumentative. Or a girl who comes in five minutes late and says she's not late today—those are the kids I go after."

Jents was a football coach before he began coaching debate, so he knows how much competition engages students. Now he sees them engaged in world issues rather than offensive strategy. "This year it's about China, and I hear students having discussions about military presence in the South China Sea being key to trade, and it's really cool because those are things that we don't necessarily get a chance to cover in the school day."

Two of his students, Jahnaya Guzman and Brandon Flowers (personal interviews, January 5, 2017), started out competing at the novice level their senior year. He soon bumped them up to the junior varsity level. "We lost every single one," Brandon says. Jahnaya thought about quitting or dropping back to the novice level, but they hit their stride at the Concordia-Moorhead tournament and later ended up winning the Urban Debate League JV championship.

A few weeks after this victory, they are in a classroom after school, prepping with the seasoned varsity debaters for their first varsity appearance at the National Speech and Debate Association district tournament. They are running an affirmative argument for green technology, Brandon explains, saying the US government should create a bilateral regulatory framework with China on green technology.

"The green tech we've been arguing is CCS, carbon capture storage, but not limiting the green technology to that," he says.

They brainstorm about what they might face at the next level.

"We ran across a team when we did green tech, and they did a card [referenced a notecard] that said global warming is good because it's how China supports its economy," Jahnaya says.

"They won't be able to support an economy when they're dead," Brandon says.

"So we just find an econ card that says China's economy is good?" Jahnaya asks.

Another varsity debater explains, "No, just find a card that says the global economy is moving toward green tech, and China won't want to be left behind."

"Oh," Jahnaya answers, taking notes.

Jahnaya never expected to be a debater; she thought it was "a nerdy thing" and was a little intimidated by the other kids on the team, but Jents recruited her because she "talks a lot," and she has a good relationship with him as a classroom teacher. She fell in love with debate, and she grew passionate about both environmental science and law, which she plans to study in college. "I like winning and I like the competition," she says. "It's something where you can actually talk about things that matter. You actually get to see both sides." Brandon jumps in, "I like to argue too, but I like to argue relevant things. I have a liking for social studies and how the world works. And [debate] feels like you're at home. I know that sounds like a cliché."

Through debate, Jahnaya and Brandon have learned how to think on their feet, how to write a coherent speech or paper quickly, and how to think critically about important issues—and they have become part of a larger community.

"We didn't know any of these kids when we came into debate, but now we're all really close to each other," Jahnaya says.

Other competitions can have the same effect, opening doors for students and engaging them in deep learning. I met Lisa Ohlemann-Warer (personal interview, June 17, 2016), a new economics teacher at Gibbs High School in St. Petersburg, Florida, at the Harvard Pre-Collegiate Economics Challenge in 2016 (http://www.hcs.harvard.edu/huea/hpec_home.php). The majority of Gibbs's students are African American and low income. The school ranks in the bottom 30 percent of Florida schools on state tests, but educators there are trying to change the school's image and the students' confidence.

Ohlemann-Warer had heard about the Harvard competition and decided it would be a great incentive for her students. "If they just get a grade, that's not really a motivation for them," she says. When she told her students about going to Harvard, they were excited but nervous. "Their self-esteem sometimes is not very high. Even though they are great kids, they don't trust themselves very much to do great things," she says. She took four girls to the competition, and they struggled against elite schools like Phillips Exeter Academy and Choate-Rosemary Hall to answer lightning-fast questions about Gini coefficients, neoclassical economics, and Nobel Prize winners, but the experience emboldened them.

On the way home, Ohlemann-Warer says, one of the girls, a senior, asked her if it was too late to apply to college. No one in her family had gone, and she was planning to join the military, but the competition changed that. "She actually applied to the University of South Florida, and she got a full scholarship. She's going to college now, and she's going to major in political science and maybe minor in economics," Ohlemann-Warer says.

The competition, which they did not win, was literally life-changing. Next time, Ohlemann-Warer says, she'll take two teams.

Kathy Whepley (personal interview, August 23, 2016), an English teacher, and her colleagues at Wichita North High School began involving their students in the Poetry Out Loud poetry slam competition a few years ago (http://www.poetryoutloud.org/). Most of her students are Hispanic, and nearly all are on free lunch; the poetry slam has helped them develop confidence and step outside their comfort zone.

The students move from in-class competition to a schoolwide competition (which draws a student audience) to regional and state levels. One of her sophomore girls, Mariela Ornelas, won the school competition with Stephen Crane's poem "In the Desert."

"She did that poem and gave me chills," Whepley said. "She's a quiet kid. She's a really amazing student, incredibly bright, incredibly articulate, but you just wouldn't think of her as a performer. I had never heard it delivered the way she did. She really got it."

Mariela says she worked really hard on not showing her nervousness while performing in front of forty to fifty of her peers. "I know last year I would shake just a little bit. This year I was like, 'OK, you need to work on that.' I didn't shake, so I was really proud of myself," she says (personal interview, February 5, 2017).

Mariela says she is not particularly competitive, but the experience was very rewarding. "I do like the fact that there's some recognition for reciting the poem," she says.

Of course, not every student wants to read poetry aloud, so Whepley said the teachers have increased the number of practice poetry recitations they do in class, to build comfort and a sense of camaraderie around it. The poetry slam becomes "a really fun day," she says. "I think it gives kids a little more ownership of what they're learning. . . . They get really intimate with the poem and become an expert."

Academic competitions also give students another opportunity to shine, especially students who might not excel in sports. Will Tjernlund, who took my class but never went on to compete in Econ Challenge, found that opportunity during our in-class economics competitions (personal interview, December 6, 2016). "I liked how I got to compete," he said. "I am not a very big or athletic person. I love to compete, but gym class was the only place in school where I could get that release. It was unfortunate, since I was so bad at sports."

But what about when students lose? How does that affect their confidence level and learning? Think about Brandon and Jahnaya, the Urban Debate League partners. They went 2-7 when they bumped up to the junior varsity level, and they thought about quitting. But they didn't.

It was a big adjustment—they had to transition from using prepackaged arguments to their own arguments, and they had to be "on the spot looking for things to run against them," Jahnaya says. Once they made that leap, they were solid.

"When you lose, it makes you want to work harder," Brandon explains. "The biggest thing I noticed is we started getting more confident, and then we started winning."

Effective coaching can change how unsuccessful competitors view themselves. We've all seen coaches, teachers, and even parents who berate children and undermine their self-worth when they do not perform well in athletic events—it is devastating to the child. But we can teach students how to win and lose graciously, and how to focus on the quality of our personal performance rather than the competitive outcome.

One of the hardest moments for me as an academic coach was seeing a team of highly prepared Econ Challenge students lose a close competition at the local level in 2014. Three of the four students (including one of my sons) had been on a team that took third place nationally the previous year, and it seemed impossible that they could be eliminated so quickly. One competition, one wrong answer, and they were done for the year.

I was never trained in how to coach students to deal with losing, but I knew I did not want them to get down on themselves. I didn't want them to blame each other or wallow in the loss. These were four talented kids, and I wanted to make sure they knew that I was not disappointed or fixated on the outcome. A few weeks later, we went to the Harvard competition (which required no qualifying) and focused on fun. We acted out historical moments on Boston's Freedom Trail. One of the students pretended to be a tour guide, telling ridiculous made-up stories. We went out for Mr. Bartley's burgers followed by ice cream followed by Insomnia Cookies. We crammed into the hotel shuttle and later into two Ubers to get downtown and back. When we got home to Minnesota, our loss was mostly forgotten. And a little over twelve months later, that team (with three of the same students) won the national competition. They were not diminished by the loss; they were motivated.

Abraham Chen, one of the four students on that team, remembers the loss as surprising but not disheartening.

"It was very humbling, so we all worked a lot harder the next year to make sure we would do well," he says. "It was really motivating, for senior year, to close it out better."

HOW DO YOU INCLUDE COMPETITION IN YOUR INSTRUCTION?

The first time I took students to a competition was on Minnesota History Day 1998. For History Day, students work in teams to pursue their own in-depth historical inquiries, linked to an annual theme like "migration" or "innovation." I was a history teacher for only two years, but I had gone to a History Day workshop the first fall, so I took students to the state competition both years. It was an amazing spectacle: table after table of in-depth primary source research and thoughtful analysis, described through museum-quality displays. It helped me realize what motivated students were capable of.

When I started teaching journalism and advising the school newspaper in 1999, I began entering my journalism students in contests and competitions, letting them see how external judges—not just their own adviser—would evaluate their work. (They were rated well at the state level, but it took thirteen years to reach the level of finalist at the prestigious National Pacemaker Awards.)

A few years later, I entered economics students in the Economics Challenge and JA Titan, and later, the Personal Finance Challenge, the JA Company Program, the International Economic Summit, and the Federal Reserve Essay Contest (mentioned in Chapter 5). I've tried others as well, like the H&R Block Budget Challenge (a complex personal finance simulation) and the local bar association's Law Day essay contest (on a civil liberties issue each year), but I gave those up—I have only so much time.

None of these competitions was difficult to find. I stumbled onto each of the competitions at conferences—or they came to me in postcards or brochures. The sponsors are constantly seeking new participants, and some even pay the expenses or send volunteers to run them on-site. What's challenging isn't finding a competition but sorting through all the options, figuring out which ones provide the most valuable learning opportunities for students, determining how to integrate them into your curriculum or club, and not getting overwhelmed like I did. There are essay contests, speech and debate meets, journalism contests, and poetry slams for English classes; robotics, Science Olympiad, CyberPatriot, Mathematics League, and a host of research competitions for science and math classes; *Shark Tank* and DECA competitions for business, economics, and entrepreneurship teachers; History Day and Academic Decathlon and Quiz Bowl for social studies—and so many more. Just google the topic you're interested in, and you will find a variety of options. Then, you need to figure out how to incorporate them.

There are four basic ways to integrate competition into high school curriculum:

- Use a competition, like JA Titan, as a one-day class activity.

- Design a class around a competition. I've done this with Econ Challenge, and I've seen other teachers design *Shark Tank*–style classes, History Day classes, or robotics classes. Mike Lampert requires all of his honors research students to prepare for the Intel Science and Engineering Fair.

- Integrate a competition into a class as part of an ongoing project. I used History Day this way, and now I use the International Economic Summit.

- Prepare students for competitions as an extracurricular, such as debate, mock trial, math team, or speech team.

When I started taking teams to Econ Challenge in 2008, I decided to design my economics class around it, and I persuaded my professional learning community colleagues to do the same. We prepared all of our 400-plus ninth-grade regular econ students for the contest, offering them "challenge assignments" and in-class activities modeled on the regional competition. We had mini in-class competitions—where students took challenge tests in class and competed in Quiz Bowl rounds—and students came up with team names and logos, like the Eco-Freakos. (These were ninth graders!)

Because the challenge tests were different from our usual tests and required strategy and speed (but didn't count for a grade), they generated a lot of excitement. They also pushed students to learn material that went well beyond the course objectives and final exam, so many intro students learned concepts like *elasticity* and *game theory* just for Econ Challenge.

Sola Olateju is an econ major at Wheaton College today mainly because of those in-class competitions years ago. "There's a certain enjoyment or drive that comes from competing with others," Sola says. "It's a very different teaching style, not like any other classes I'd had before that. It made anything I had to learn for it something I wanted to do" (personal interview, October 26, 2016).

Sola qualified for one of the regional competition teams as a freshman, and vividly remembers missing school to go to the University of St. Thomas and later to the Federal Reserve Bank of Minneapolis. "People dress up professionally, you meet professionals who do economics for a living, and there's a chance to realize there are other high schools out there, other bright students," he says. "You think, 'Wow, I thought I was really good before, but there is so much more I could know.' It raises the bar about what is possible."

When I stopped teaching regular econ, I changed Econ Challenge to an extracurricular activity. Now the AP students meet weekly before school and sometimes on the weekends, and they work on practice tests and coach each other. They also run most of the practices for the students on the regular-level team, who come from other econ teachers' classes. When competition season starts in March, both teams start devoting more hours to it. In their practices, they figure out ways to explain difficult concepts to each other, only rarely bringing questions to me. The leaders take pride in being able to help younger students understand.

"I think a lot of people's perception of competition is very cutthroat, but when you're working toward a common goal, it becomes more collaborative," Abraham Chen says.

Here's an exchange from one of the AP team's practices in 2017:

A new member: For number 11, since it says the marginal product of labor is twice as high as for wheat, wouldn't that imply that you're able to produce more corn . . . thus you're able to charge a higher price?

One of the captains: But remember, it says the value of the marginal product is equal for both of them. If the marginal product they're producing is twice as high, the price has to be twice as low because the total value of everything you produce is equal.

Another student: If it helps, I think of it . . . The value of marginal product of labor is easier to think of as MRP.

The new student nods his head, and they move on.

Jacob Weightman and Abraham Chen, who were both on the team that won the National Econ Challenge in 2015, believe preparing for Econ Challenge this way taught them to study for deep understanding, rather than to get a good grade on a test. It was important to know what they were talking about, so they could explain things to each other.

Abraham says Econ Challenge helped prepare him for difficult tests in college. At the University of California–Berkeley, he said, you can't just take for granted that professors will tell you everything you need to know; you have to keep pushing and adding to your own knowledge. "I think what is the most rewarding feeling at Berkeley and at Econ Challenge is when you do problems you were doing a few months earlier and you think, 'Oh, this is really easy,'" he says. "To see that transition shows a lot of progress. You struggle a lot to push it uphill. For technical classes, you look back and it almost feels like a part of you that you've gained physically. In high school, you could usually push your way through a test and then forget about it. Competition makes you have a more comprehensive mentality to studying."

Figures 7.1 to 7.3 show students, including Jacob and Abraham, competing in Econ Challenge. (See Figures 7.1–7.3.)

Figure 7.1
Abraham Chen, Emily Ruan, and Jacob Weightman answer quiz bowl questions
in the 2015 Minnesota Economics Challenge. They won the state championship
and went on to win the National Economics Challenge.

Figure 7.2
Jacob Weightman, Emily Ruan, Abraham Chen, and Sam Rush pose for photos
with their trophy after winning the 2015 Minnesota Economics Challenge.

Figure 7.3
Ben Chen and Abhishek Vijayakumar work through a challenging problem in the team round of the 2017 Minnesota Economics Challenge.

Another competition I've integrated into my class—in a slightly different way—is the International Economic Summit, managed by Boise State University (econsummit.org). The Summit requires students to work in groups of three to five to learn about one nation and represent it in a one-day simulated trade summit. It's cleverly organized, so that some students represent wealthy nations like Germany and Canada, while others represent middle-income countries like Argentina, and others poor countries like Uganda. Every country has to meet its goals, but the goals differ. Some countries have a lot of oil to trade, while others have more tourism or technology. The students need to figure out who to build strategic alliances with, who to trade with, and how to invest in their own country's capital. It's like a strategy board game come to life.

During the semester, students create detailed resource maps (see Figures 7.4 and 7.5), research economic data like GDP, inflation, and currency values, and learn about their nation's trade patterns to prepare for the summit. Everything we learn in macro, they apply. We come back to it every few weeks, and the actual summit day comes after the AP test in May. It's a day of colorful displays and costumes, lots of food sampling, loud negotiations, and chaos.

In 2016, my colleague and I surveyed students on whether they found the summit valuable and what they learned from it. Ninety percent of our 120 AP Macro students recommended doing it again, and 50 percent said it taught them to strategize. Here's some of their advice for future summit participants:

> *Make sure to figure out which resources are scarce*
> *before planning your import goals. We missed a*
> *goal because of a small supply and high demand for*
> *military goods.*

> *Be assertive during your trading, and don't*
> *waste time.*

> *DO NOT procrastinate! DO NOT pick a group*
> *based on your friend circle; focus on a person's*
> *devotion to what they do. DO NOT let your group*
> *push you around. Pick a leader WHO KNOWS*
> *WHAT THEY ARE DOING AND HAVE RESPECT*
> *FOR EVERYONE'S DECISIONS AND OPINIONS!!*

Nate Moller, whose team represented Taiwan, says they decided to create a spreadsheet for their alliance, spelling out who would trade resources with whom and creating a powerful oligopoly. "It was challenging, the whole logistics of trading with everybody and not knowing what everybody was going to do," he says (personal interview, January 26, 2017).

Vivian Gao, whose team represented Indonesia, said they managed to meet all of their trade goals, despite being a less developed country. They tried to get one of the wealthy countries to give them a foreign aid grant, but the wealthy countries were trying to get poor countries to pay for them, which was frustrating. She loved the competitive aspect of it: "I think the whole atmosphere surrounding the summit, it was electric" (personal interview, January 26, 2016).

Figure 7.4
AP Macro students Kimie Shen and Chloe Wick created this resource map of South Korea for their booth at our high school's 2017 International Economic Summit.

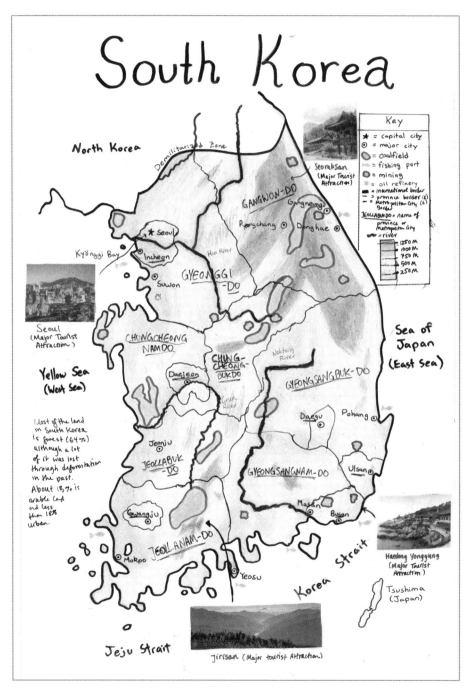

One of the most popular—and growing—high school competitions is robotics. In 2016, more than 3,000 teams including more than 78,000 students participated in FIRST Robotics (https://www.firstinspires.org) alone (there are several organizations), and 600 teams from twenty nations competed in the FIRST global championship. One of these teams was Knight-Krawler from Irondale High School (also in my district), which has made it to nationals the last four years.

Figure 7.5
AP Macro students Emily Feng, Deepta Jasthi, Jenna Stellmack, and Sandy Zhang created this resource map of Singapore for their booth at our high school's 2017 International Economic Summit.

Neely Drake, a team captain, says robotics requires that students with a lot of different skill sets collaborate over an intensive period of several months. Some students build the robots; some make pieces for the robots, using CAD and 3-D printers; some program the robots; some drive the robots; some do public relations and seek grant money for the team; and some scout out other teams to decide who to form alliances with at competitions. "You can't really build a 120-pound robot by yourself," Neely says (personal interviews, December 12, 2016, and January 7, 2017).

Neely was one of forty students gathered at school on a frigid Saturday morning in January for the "big reveal"—the announcement of the FIRST Robotics challenge for 2017. A video streamed simultaneously to teams around the world, showing a virtual walk-through of the competition and then outlining all of the detailed specs. At the end, students were given a code to access the contest manual. The KnightKrawler team would need to build and program several small robots, each capable of shooting eight to ten whiffle balls per second into goals whose top width was 21.5 inches, delivering gears to an "airship," and climbing itself up a rope.

After the video, the team split into groups, and Neely led the group reading about match play and safety rules. She created a Google Doc for shared notes, and the students settled in around a library table with their laptops.

"You're not allowed to launch a gear; you can't throw them," she tells the group.

"You can't drop your battery on the field and leave it behind," another student adds.

"And there's rules for the rope you can bring," Neely says.

"Oh, we can't hack networks. 'No team or team member shall interfere or attempt to interfere with any other team's networks.' We also can't set up a wireless network. . . . And during the match you can't touch your banner."

Neely imitates reaching up to touch a banner. "Whoops!"

They're having fun, sharing their responses to nitpicky rules as well as challenges—"They're not going to have enough gears; if every team gets one or two! It's so dumb that if they don't count the fuel fast enough, you don't get scored for it"—and their camaraderie will help them through the intensity of the next twelve weeks.

During build season, Neely said, she'll spend about thirteen hours a week on robotics, with meetings on Mondays, Wednesdays, Fridays, and all day Saturday. "Toward the end of build season, we're really crunching for time, so people will stay till, like, midnight."

Neely said she'd enjoy working on robots even without the competitive aspect, but knowing you are preparing for a contest adds an important element, pushing everyone to work their hardest.

Ben Young, KnightKrawler's build team captain, says the competitions have a great atmosphere—highly energized, but not brutal like soccer, which he also plays (personal interview, December 14, 2016). "They're not one team against another team—you can be with this team in one match, and then in another match against them," he says. "There's no hard feelings or anything. They're all about 'gracious professionalism,' and you get teams that aren't good getting help from the top teams at regionals."

In one competition, the KnightKrawler team helped a team from mainland China rebuild their robot on the spot. "The amount of joy they had when their robot was on the field and actually moved during that match, it was a sight to see," Ben says.

And yet, he still sees the competitive aspect as vital. "I'm very competitive," he says. "The competition was actually what first drew me to the team."

WHAT ARE THE CHALLENGES OF USING COMPETITION?

Competition can potentially lead to bad outcomes: students who feel discouraged by losing, students who are cut from a team, students who don't find their niche. I get it. I was cut from almost everything I tried out for in junior high and high school: cheerleading, pompom squad, volleyball, tennis. I was never quite coordinated enough for anything that required physical skill, and it was discouraging.

That's why it's so important that we offer diverse opportunities for students to join teams—some of which don't "cut"—and it's why we need to incorporate competition into our classrooms rather than just in extracurriculars. I can't take every student to Econ Challenge; I'm limited to two teams of four students at the first level of competition. That's why I loved incorporating the challenge in my class, so every student got to play. We can include almost every student at our school in JA Titan, and we do. The only students left out are ones who skip regular economics to go straight to the AP class, and they can participate if they take AP Microeconomics. All the AP Macroeconomics students participate in the Federal Reserve Essay Contest. Similarly, Kathy Whepley at Wichita North includes all of her AP language students in classroom poetry slams, even those who don't sign up to participate in the schoolwide, regional, or state contests. (North has six sections of AP, which include a diverse population.) She has also used it with lower-ability kids, who struggled to read poetry, and would like to get them more involved. "I think what I would need to do differently with them is really work on matching them with a poem they can relate to and really understand," she says (personal interview, August 23, 2016).

Another challenge of incorporating competition is learning how to coach without overemphasizing winning. We have to teach our students resilience, and we have to make sure they develop a sense of perspective. FIRST Robotics offers an excellent method to do this, with its focus on "gracious professionalism." Neely explains it this way: "Sometimes losing is not the greatest thing, but you have to accept it. And if you win, you can't go and brag about it to other people. You have to be nice, and say, 'Oh, it was nice playing against you.'" That's why the KnightKrawler team didn't hesitate to help the Chinese team whose robot didn't work. They don't want to beat someone who is struggling; they want to do their best against other good teams.

How a coach deals with losing is also incredibly powerful. A few years ago, a top team at the National Econ Challenge did surprisingly poorly in the written rounds of competition. No one could understand what had happened—were their answers scored improperly? They were upset, but at the end of the competition day, when all the teams got off a boat cruise at Chelsea Pier to head back to the hotel, their coach took them to the batting cages and the ice rink for a night of fun activities instead. That's the kind of thing that helps students learn perspective and start to value the team, and the camaraderie, over winning.

Of course, time and resources are a huge challenge for any academic coach. Many teachers are exhausted at the end of the school day and just want to get home, especially knowing that a pile of work is waiting to be graded. And those who coach sports teams are already occupied for hours after school. Teachers who involve students in academic competition need to put in extra time and sometimes for little or no extra pay. "I tell people my teaching day doesn't start until the bell rings at the end of the day," Lampert says. "That's when I do a lot of coaching."

It sounds clichéd, but the intangible rewards do make it worthwhile. When students are excited about learning, you don't want to shut it down. How can I not take time for a student like Abraham, when he comes in after school to show me a problem about taxes and consumer surplus and to ask for help figuring it out? I've had days when my room was bustling for hours after school with journalism students editing on one side, while students were doing practice problems for Econ Challenge in one corner and strategizing for JA Company in another corner. That energy—it's what all teachers want, all the time.

It is possible to keep the coaching burden manageable by training student captains to actually act as leaders. Most of the time, my advanced students run practices and company meetings, not me. I'm there to supervise, but I'm often multitasking and prepping or grading papers until they have a question for me. I saw the same thing with the debaters at St. Paul Central: Jents, the coach, was working with the video-game club in the room next door, while the more experienced varsity debaters helped Jahnaya and Brandon with their preparation.

I know many teachers have a hard time finding the funding to attend competitions, which can also be a huge barrier. Even paying for transportation—when buses can cost three hundred dollars for a day—or finding a sub can make it challenging to attend an out-of-school contest. Administrative support for academic competitions is critical. I've been lucky to work in a school where administrators value extracurriculars and see them as an important way to connect to and motivate students. Lisa Ohlemann-Warer is lucky, too. She never would have been able to bring her St. Petersburg, Florida, kids to the Harvard Pre-Collegiate Economics Challenge without strong support from her principal and school board; the students couldn't afford to pay their own way.

For many teachers, the support of outside organizations is also critical. A lot of companies want to contribute to education as part of their charitable giving, and we can tap into that. Junior Achievement provides business volunteers to run Titan and mentor students in JA Company. Neely's robotics team has worked to find local sponsors like Medtronic, the Groves Foundation, and the Best Buy Children's Foundation, who provide funding as well as mentors to help teach skills like coding and CADing. Writing grants is one of the official roles on the team, just as it is for many nonprofits in the real world. When the team makes it to nationals, "the sponsors pay for a lot of the trip," making it affordable for students, she says.

TIPS FOR TEACHERS

How do I get started if I have never used competition?

- Just do it! I had received postcards for years from the Minnesota Council on Economic Education before I finally decided to take a team to a competition. I never thought my students would be interested, and I wasn't sure they'd perform well. It's not like I even taught every concept on those competition tests. Once we did it, though, we were hooked. My regular students won their regional competition and went to State, and several of them couldn't wait to come back for the AP team.

- Be a student of the competition. When you are there, pay attention, take notes, ask lots of questions, and debrief the students who go to find out what they wish they'd known. I kept the released tests and took notes on the Quiz Bowl questions, so I'd be ready for coaching the following year.

- If there's training, take advantage of it. I'm currently involved in training other teachers who haven't participated in Econ Challenge, giving them tips and free materials. If you can find a mentor or another team to observe, take advantage of it and learn everything you can from them.

- Avoid anything costly. Start small and build from there. Econ Challenge charges no entrance fees, and the sponsors pay for T-shirts and meals on-site. If you make it to higher levels of competition, they pay the travel expenses, too.

- Use competition in class, not just as an outside reward for a few kids. Anne Marciano (personal interview, August 24, 2016), a math teacher in New Jersey, uses a "trig wars" competition to help her students memorize the value of trigonometric functions. The students make notecards and play a game similar to the card game War–two students put down cards, and whoever's card is bigger takes the pair. For example, tan 45 (1) beats sin 30 ($1/2$), but you have to know the values to know if you win. "As we move through the year, the cards multiply until we have 120–150," she said. "We have a double-elimination tournament."

How can I build on my use of competition to encourage deeper understanding and content learning?

- Network with other teachers, at conferences or through social media, to find out about effective, meaningful competitions. Vet everything to make sure it actually meets objectives that are important to you, your class, your school. I wasn't sure I wanted to keep doing Econ Challenge, which uses a lot of multiple-choice tests, until I realized that students were digging deep to prepare for it. The questions require a lot of knowledge, application, and analytical thinking–they are not simply vocabulary terms.

- Focus on competitions that promote teamwork and collaboration, and encourage students coaching students. Sometimes students teaching students gets a bad rep, like the more advanced students are wasting their time, but in team situations kids are intrinsically motivated to help others.

- Find out from the students–what are they learning? What could they be learning? Econ Challenge students regularly surpass my knowledge of economics, which I think is cool but some teachers might find intimidating. When they ask questions I can't answer, I'm happy to turn to colleagues and professors I've met through CEE (Council for Economic Education) to find answers.

How will I assess and know if it's effective?

- Measure changes in performance and attitude in classes where you introduce competition. In the years I used the Econ Challenge model in introductory economics, I don't think a single student failed the class. There were kids who struggled, but the energy seemed to sweep them all along like a current.

- Survey the students, like we did with the International Economic Summit. We asked the students six questions, including, How would you rate the summit as an educational activity? What was the most valuable aspect of the summit? If you did the summit again, what would you like to spend more time on?

- Take your results in a local or regional competition as useful feedback. How did your students perform? Were they comparable to peers from other schools? Where were they lacking in skills or knowledge? My students won the regular-level local Econ Challenge on our first outing, but we struggled for years to compete at the AP level. Frequently, I didn't know how to answer or explain many of the questions, but I learned a lot and improved my instruction (for all students) by participating and asking questions.

8

AUTHENTIC TASKS: ENCOURAGE WORK THAT MATTERS OUTSIDE SCHOOL

During her senior year of high school, Samantha Kalsow wanted the Synergy Club to sponsor a "Bike to School Day." The principal said no. There wasn't a protected bike lane or continuous sidewalk, and the school didn't want to support an activity that put students at risk (personal interview, October 10, 2016).

Samantha brainstormed with a friend who had been injured in a bike accident at a nearby intersection—he had jumped over a fence at a state highway— and they decided they wanted to tackle the bigger problem: the lack of safe bike trails in the community. But they weren't sure where to start. I suggested they try the state legislature.

Over the following months, Samantha and her friend took on the legislative process. They e-mailed legislators, polled students and teachers, gathered signatures on a petition, printed enlarged Google maps showing the dangerous intersection, teamed up with the American Red Cross, spent hours preparing and practicing speeches, and ultimately testified before Minnesota's House and Senate transportation committees on the "Safe Routes to School" bill.

In a hearing on the bill, they explained the problem, shared their maps and visual images, and told personal stories to make their point. "One of our friends also bikes to school fairly regularly, and she often has to lift her bike up over a guardrail, which also poses a safety concern," Samantha told the committee, pointing out the guardrail in a picture.

They impressed the committee, and they got their paved bike path (part of the community's sidewalk system). They also learned an incredible amount about the legislative process and personal efficacy.

"Every time I go past that sidewalk, I take a little bit of ownership of it," Samantha says. "That's my sidewalk. To actually have an influence on a piece of legislation and government being just a high school student was amazing."

Samantha was a serious student before the bike path project, but the opportunity to do real work that mattered to her was highly motivating, much more so than routine schoolwork. She estimates they spent fifty-plus hours on the project in their spare time senior year.

"It was something close to home," she explains. "Everybody knew that missing piece of sidewalk. We both had internal motivation because we wanted to bike to school. The fact that we couldn't . . . It was our own drive."

WHAT ARE AUTHENTIC TASKS?

Early Saturday afternoon on New Year's Eve day, seven students are huddled around a table at the local community center. Behind them, workers are decorating for a New Year's Eve party, but the students are focused on their laptop screens and the work ahead: how to reduce costs, set prices, improve marketing, and keep up production.

"The Christmas pouches didn't sell as well as the pencil bags," Nandini Avula tells the group (group interviews, December 31, 2016, and January 9, 2017). "If we could think of any ways to make the pencil bags more efficiently, that's one thing we could improve on. Do you think we need more zippers?"

"Yes, we need more white and black zippers," says Yoo-Jin Hwang.

"Can you order more?" Nandini says, looking to her left at Shelley Wang. "Uh-huh."

"And I was thinking of maybe setting quotas within departments. With production, do you think you guys could make four bags per week?" Nandini asks.

"Each?" answers Shriparna Patnayak.

"Yes, and if you can't make the bags because you don't have a sewing machine, maybe cut rectangles?"

Like Samantha, these students are immersed in their work. Running SaySew—producing and selling custom-made pencil pouches—isn't just a school project for them. It's a real business, and they have to worry about customers and inventory and price points and sales strategies. They have to decide whether to set up an Etsy site, and whether they can keep up with demand if they do. They can't always take days off.

"You can't just procrastinate and put it to the side," Nandini says later. "You're still going to get more orders, and you need to sell more. You have to keep track of everything; everything is like a domino effect. If we don't have the product, we can't take the pictures, and if we can't take the pictures, we can't do marketing."

"And if we don't have zippers, we can't make the product," Shriparna adds, laughing. "A class can only take you so far in learning about business and entrepreneurship. Here, you just learn as you go."

What these students are doing—and what Samantha did—is an authentic task. Authentic tasks are real work, work that has meaning outside the four walls of school. Students doing authentic tasks might also be writing letters to the editor, conducting their own scientific research, writing music, producing newspapers or TV shows, creating educational films or PSAs, or producing apps.

I've used authentic tasks with my students since my first years teaching middle school English in Wichita. Because I had worked outside of academia as a journalist, I thought contact with the "real world" would be motivating to teenagers, who long to be seen as capable young adults. It was.

Authentic tasks are work with real-world implications, and they are so immersive that students lose track of time, forget about getting graded, and stop drawing a line between school and fun. Ask students why they work so hard when a task is authentic, and they say, "It matters," "People are counting on me," "We're a family."

Katrina Renacia, one of my *Viewer* newspaper editors in 2015–16, described it this way: "I had fun editing stories. The whole thing was just really fun for me; it was just a hobby. I worked on it everywhere; that's why

I had Google Drive on my phone, so I could edit anywhere. I've definitely edited at the mall. That's why I had to convince my parents to get me an iPhone for data" (personal interview, January 4, 2017).

Authentic tasks are similar to project-based learning, which is growing in popularity in American schools, but they are not exactly the same. School projects are not necessarily meaningful in the outside world; students researching the Plague might prepare a poster diagramming the spread of the disease, but only for a classroom audience. Likewise, a task might be authentic without being a full-blown project. When my eighth graders wrote letters to the editor of the *Wichita Eagle* asking the city to build them a new skate park, or when my editor in chief Sisi Wei (personal interview, December 16, 2016) skipped her AP French test to make calls and find a new printing company for the *Viewer* (when the old one announced it was going out of business), those were not projects; the work was real. A business plan might be enough for a *project*, but launching the business makes it an *authentic task*.

Students like Samantha and Nandini often get involved in authentic tasks on their own, outside school or through extracurriculars. Some students at my school write video games or make movies on their own or work on political campaigns or start bakeries or create handmade jewelry. But not every student gets those opportunities, especially if their parents don't know how to work the system, or if they lack startup funds, home Internet access, or transportation, which can be true for many children in poverty and recent immigrants. Many students are so busy working minimum-wage jobs during the week that they wouldn't have time to think about starting their own enterprise or getting involved in legislative action. This is why we need to make these learning experiences part of a high school education.

When we do, we need to make sure we are giving students an authentic experience, not just a sandbox experience. That means we must give them the opportunity to speak their own minds and spread their wings, challenge perceived injustices and develop efficacy—and we have to give them the chance to fail. It's too easy for teachers to manufacture a make-believe political experience, where an elected official comes to class to talk with them, rather than having students initiate contact and possibly be ignored. (I advised my students never to tell anyone they were doing a "school project," and most followed that.) It's also too easy for teachers to create make-believe business experiences, where the teacher helps design a product or service, provides a captive audience for sales, and absorbs any losses—like a class car wash or bake sale.

Authentic tasks require students to put themselves out there, to take risks. They have to call the legislator's office or the potential customer's office.

They have to ask the difficult questions or make a good sales pitch. They have to resolve conflicts, sometimes with their own team members. This is scary for them, but it's also empowering.

For Katrina, it was a huge confidence booster. She moved to Minnesota from the Philippines as a sophomore, and though she already spoke English, she had a heavy accent. "People kept asking me to keep repeating the words I was saying. That was a confidence buzzkill," she says. But when she started interviewing students and teachers as a reporter for the *Viewer*, it boosted her confidence. "I could now talk to people without cringing or shaking."

Authentic tasks require students to stand on their own, but they still need support from teachers. Our role is to create a conducive environment, help students identify appropriate challenges, and provide them with knowledge, tips, and skills. We know how to identify the right legislators. We know how to present ourselves in an interview. We know how to talk to potential customers. We also have to try to keep well-intentioned adults (including ourselves) from interfering—as long as the students are following laws and school rules.

WHY USE AUTHENTIC TASKS?

When I was twenty-two, just out of college and working as a reporter for the *Wichita Eagle*, I had to call Bob Dole. That might not sound like a big deal, but this was not long before he ran for president, and he was a significant power broker in the US Senate. I was at work on a Saturday afternoon (July 8, 1989, to be exact), and Rep. Dan Glickman, a Kansas Democrat, had just announced he was refusing honoraria. I was supposed to get Sen. Dole's reaction.

My editor assured me: he never answers our calls.

So I called and left a message, and of course, Bob Dole called me back. Here's how the conversation went, more or less:

> **Me:** *Hello, this is Martha Sevetson at the* Wichita Eagle.
>
> **Bob Dole:** *Martha? Bob Dole here.*
>
> *(Ten seconds of silence. My heart racing.)*
>
> **Me:** *Oh, yes, I called you—*
>
> **Bob Dole:** *What about?*

> *Me:* Dan Glickman announced he's no longer going to take honoraria—
>
> *Bob Dole:* So what?

That's what I remember. He was gruff and impatient, and I was nervous. I had never interviewed anyone famous or powerful at the national level before. I ended the call after a few more minutes feeling like a novice, but I had my reaction quote.

At some point, all of us have to learn how to be adults. Not only that, we have to learn to regard other adults as our peers, as people we can work with, rather than as people we are simply expected to obey. We have to realize that sometimes adults are wrong, that sometimes we need to question decisions and speak up for ourselves to effect change. That's a hard lesson, especially when high school students have been taught for so long just to follow the rules. I was still learning it at age twenty-two, when I made that phone call.

Anna Brockway learned this lesson at a much younger age, working on our student newspaper, the *Viewer* (personal interview, December 28, 2016). In November of her senior year, Anna was leaving school one day and saw police officers searching a car in the school parking lot. The next day, the school was abuzz with rumors about the search. A student's phone was searched. Free speech was infringed. A backpack was taken. Drugs were involved.

"I was a student, and normally I would have just been one of the students who maybe would have been affected in some way, maybe outraged over the phone [search]," she says. "Being on the *Viewer* put me in direct contact with the school administration and the police department and the DEA, which gave me more perspective about what was happening and allowed me in some ways to bridge the divide between those people and the way their duties affected the school community."

Anna interviewed school administrators, who wouldn't tell her much— and didn't particularly want to see the story in the student newspaper. She interviewed students, including some who had been drug buyers. She left school one day to drive to the local sheriff's office and obtain the incident report, which told the story in great detail. According to her published story, the report said the vehicle "contained suspected marijuana, suspected cocaine, suspected mushrooms, 9 pills of suspected Ecstasy, 1 digital scale, and $265." She also interviewed a DEA agent, who called it "a pretty significant arrest" (Brockway 2007).

Anna wasn't just being a student journalist—she was working as a real journalist, doing all the work that journalists do. Not only that, she had to stand up to pressure not to run the story; she had to risk offending school authorities who had power over her. She learned how to ask difficult questions, how to respectfully challenge authority, and how to manage the stress of it all. I supported her and gave her suggestions, like where to get the police report, but I let her take the lead. She talked to the administrators and the DEA on her own. It was seriously empowering. "I felt like I was kind of being the voice of the students," she says. (See Anna's story, Chapter 8, Sample 1, in the appendix.)

The next time Anna found herself in a similar position, writing an article that upset authorities on her college campus, she knew how to deal with the fallout. She was prepared to stand up for herself, and she stayed poised. "I think the only reason I could do that was because of my experiences in the *Viewer* and having some practice dealing with the administration there," she says. "*Viewer* was really the first place I had to express your opinion and get involved in the community in a way that was actually productive."

What Anna was doing when she reported on the drug bust was far from contrived. Instead, it involved what Daniel Pink (2012), who has written extensively about motivation, calls the three keys: autonomy, mastery, and purpose. She was doing work that was deeply important to her, and she developed excellent reporting and writing skills in the process.

Building this kind of confidence and assertiveness is one key reason for engaging students in authentic tasks, but it's not the only reason. Authentic tasks are important because they are deeply engaging and motivating to students. They give many students a reason to care about school and a taste of what they can do after high school. They can also be used to teach valuable academic content and skills as well as leadership, collaboration, creativity, and job skills—some of the critical 21st century skills.

When Josh Jones was a freshman in my economics class, he wasn't particularly motivated (personal interview, January 9, 2017). He was up out of his seat all the time, constantly in motion, constantly distracting everyone. If he wasn't in motion, he was asleep. He was a friendly kid, but he drove me crazy—and he knows this.

"I don't know why I wasn't interested in school—maybe because it was overwhelming to me; I didn't know how to accomplish tasks in a timely manner," he says. "I think that changed when I was given things that I wanted to do." Junior year, Josh quit playing sports, which he hadn't really liked anyway, and joined the *Viewer* and theater. He started taking classes such as humanities and philosophy, which helped him think about life and develop a sense of purpose. And he fell in love with the art of page design.

Senior year Josh worked out a schedule where he could spend three hours a day in the newspaper office, perfecting pages in Adobe InDesign, choosing the right fonts, resizing photos, figuring out how to play each story. "Given, I wasn't working all of those three hours," he says. "But it made it easy to work. If I had an idea, I could work on it. If I had something big, I could work on it the whole time."

By the time he graduated from high school, Josh was transformed. He was passionate and focused; his energy was funneled into his work, not frittered around the room. He wanted to talk about design ideas, wanted to meet leaders in the field (I helped him attend a professional workshop with design guru Tim Harrower), and he wanted to do well in his other classes to prepare himself for college.

Josh said it wasn't necessarily the news that drove him, or even the sense of a real audience reading his work, but the knowledge that other people on staff were counting on him, that what he did was vital. "People are depending on you—you want this to succeed and so do they," he said. "We really wanted to make it good. People need something that feels special to them; this is mine."

Two years out of college, Josh is a designer at the Minneapolis *Star-Tribune*, and he's frequently in charge of designing the Sunday front page for half a million subscribers. He still funnels all of his energy into his work, and he meets serious deadlines, and he loves it.

Not everyone is going to find their calling in high school, but through authentic tasks, every student can experience a real-world challenge and develop a sense of efficacy. For fifteen years, I required every student in Civil Liberties (and later, the required US Government class) to work in a group on a public policy project. This involved researching a current issue—global, national, state, or local—and involving themselves in the public discourse in some way, much like Samantha did. Some students advocated for or against building new stadiums (for the Twins, Vikings, and University of Minnesota Gophers), by writing letters or marching at a local intersection with protest signs. One group attended a human trafficking seminar, then signed a petition and wrote a letter to Senator Al Franken. One group went to the school board, asking the district to add more AP classes for students. Others involved themselves in issues like same-sex marriage, bullying, the war in Iraq, and school lunch policies. The students had to decide what issue they were interested in, figure out who was in charge of making decisions, and find a way to influence the process. (See another example of student work from a public policy

project in Appendix B, Chapter 8, Sample 2, available online at sten.pub/
beatboredom.)

Zach Roozen's passion was sleep—or lack of it. He was a runner in high
school, so much of the year he was in the community pool at 6:00 a.m. for
an "aqua jog" before driving to school. He had scheduled a first-hour study
hall, assuming that would help him get some rest, but he quickly learned that
sleep was forbidden in study hall. So was skipping. Overtired and trapped
in a silent, controlled classroom, he got angry (personal interview, January
6, 2017).

"I'd wake up at 5:30 and I didn't have a class until second period [at
8:30], and I had to be there. . . . We had to be silent, that was one of the rules.
Class would start, and the kids were, like, coloring in coloring books, and I
was like, 'What are you doing?'" he says. "It wasn't what I thought a free
hour should be. I remember thinking extra sleep in the morning or being
able to consume the time the way I wanted was way more important." Zach
worked with a friend to circulate a petition; then they wrote to all the school
board members, asking them to let students take a first-hour study hall "off
campus." Although he didn't get immediate results, he felt like people listened to him, and that was empowering. He realized he could be a leader, and
he could advocate for himself.

In college, this experience shaped him in two ways—it led him to write
a major paper on "form versus substance" in education, and it empowered
him to challenge campus administrators on policies he found absurd. For
example, students in his program at the University of Southern California
are training to be actors, but they are forbidden to miss class for acting jobs.
"We get in these heated battles," he says. "What I learned in the project we
did is that a problem is like an onion. You've got all the different layers. Now
I have an approach that I know can work, through trial and error. Something
like this project allows us to figure out the framework for that."

Zach graduated high school in 2012, not knowing what impact his efforts
would have on our school. The very next year, study hall disappeared, and
students were given permission to spend free hours in the library, which has
since transformed into an open, collaborative work space with a coffee shop
and a makerspace. Now, the school board is also planning to push back start
times to help teenagers meet their need for sleep. Zach wasn't the cause of
these changes, but his voice (and other students' voices) helped.

Sometimes, authentic tasks require an unusual degree of student leadership. Earlier I mentioned Sisi, who skipped an AP test to find a new printer
for the *Viewer*. I didn't even find out she missed that test until several years
later (and I wouldn't have wanted her to)—she had just assumed finding a

printer was her responsibility. Looking back, she said she loved being treated like an adult. "As editor in chief, I look back at the things I was able to do and take responsibility for, and I'm blown away: creating an entire editorial calendar, proofing twelve pages biweekly, discussing orders with professional printers, speaking in front of reporters, enforcing deadlines. . . . I absolutely loved it," she says.

Another editor in chief, Christina Xia, found herself with even greater responsibilities—dealing with lawyers and the professional media when her group of student editors faced a prior review battle (personal interview, December 29, 2016). In Christina's senior year, our school principal objected to a story that mentioned disciplinary action against several students and tried to block distribution of the paper, but the reporter got parent permission to use the students' names, so the principal backed down. After the story came out, the principal announced that she planned to review all future issues before they went to press. Christina found herself fighting for student press freedom and ended up in a limelight she had never sought. "I think I was mostly stressed out," she says. "It was something I felt, like, as an eighteen-year-old, you really don't know what to do."

In that situation, my ability to help the editors was curtailed. Students have free speech rights, but teachers don't have the same rights, so colleagues from other schools cautioned me that I had to stay out of the legal fray or risk my job. I had no good option but to let the students make their own decisions. They had meetings in the classroom when I was at lunch, and they met with a lawyer outside of school. The superintendent called them into a private meeting with him, which made them all nervous. Under Christina's leadership, the students decided not to submit to prior review—they didn't print a paper for six weeks, basically going on strike. In the end, after a lengthy negotiation, the district agreed to a new policy without prior review.

Dealing with unhappy administrators, some negative local press coverage, and an actual legal case was not anything Christina had expected—she was an incredibly positive, nice people pleaser, not at all rebellious by nature, but she says now it was a powerful learning experience. "I think it made me realize that there are places and things that you need to stand up for, even if you are completely not comfortable with what is happening and feel like you're helpless," she says. "You can't just have people with authority—when you're right, especially—you can't just let them trample over you. It doesn't matter if you're not an adult or if you're a student."

What academic skills and content can students learn from authentic tasks? Clearly, they can learn reporting, writing, design, and editing. They can learn persuasive writing by writing letters to officials, editorials, and advertising material. They can also learn research—how to extract relevant factual information and data from nonfiction sources—and presentation skills from tasks like the public policy project.

The students involved in SaySew, the student-run business, have also learned how to do market research and analyze customer data. They have learned how to manage a budget, shop around for low-cost resources, hire employees, plan meetings, create an online store, manage a business bank account, and write up an annual report. In their several years of involvement in running Junior Achievement companies, they have also learned how to cope with frustration when communication breaks down, when team members don't pull their weight, and when there are conflicts about the direction of the company. Several of the students, including Nandini and Shelley, were involved in an earlier company that succeeded in JA competitions but fell apart behind the scenes when students just couldn't resolve disagreements over who owned intellectual property. The company disbanded, with several of the participants no longer speaking to each other.

"I think there was a lot of miscommunication and misunderstanding," Shelley says.

"And a lack of trust among members," Nandini adds. "I think trust is really important if you're trying to work together."

The next time around, with SaySew, Shelley says, "We knew what to avoid." They built their next company with a heavy emphasis on collaboration, communication, and working together on every task. "This weekend I made my first sale, even though I'm not in marketing," Shelley adds.

Authentic tasks are also a powerful way to teach science and technology. With support from teachers, students can develop their own scientific questions and conduct real research, which can be presented at conferences or competitions and published in journals. Mike Lampert, the Salem, Oregon, physics teacher, works with his Honors Research students to develop projects for multiple science and engineering fairs. His students love the chance to do real research on subjects that interest them.

Eleanor Fadely, one of Lampert's students, took the class twice and worked on several team research projects for the Toshiba Exploravision (http://www.exploravision.org/) competition, which requires students to create a hypothetical invention using future technology (personal interview, December 23, 2016). Her team decided to work on medical technology, which required learning a lot on their own about current medical technology.

"We were interested in doing something that would help people with pacemakers not have to have surgery so often to replace the batteries, a quantum bioengine," she says. "It would use temperature differentials in your body to create an electrical current that would power the pacemaker/defibrillator." The team had to create a prototype of their product, as well as a website and informational video. They spent all of spring break at school working on it. "One night, we stayed at school until one in the morning working on this project," she says.

Another year, Eleanor's group researched how to make concrete more environmentally friendly by having it reflect or absorb sunlight, depending on the season. Not surprisingly, she is now a science major at Carleton College, and she recently completed field research on landmass in Greenland. She said getting the chance to do real science in high school is what set her on this career path. "If you're going to be a scientist in the real world, problems don't appear as just formulas you have to solve on the page," Eleanor says. "They appear in real-life contexts, and you have to break them down into manageable parts."

Another benefit of authentic tasks is that they foster creativity and divergent thinking, skills that are often lost when we overemphasize right answers and facts that can be memorized for multiple-choice tests. One of my student-run businesses tried to develop a school-bus tracking app; another tried to sell 3-D printed items, like Valentine's hearts. Neither one worked at the time, and that was OK. They were good ideas, and they forced the students to try something, talk to people, develop a prototype, practice divergent thinking. The majority of entrepreneurial ventures don't work out—and that's part of the lesson.

In AP Psychology, my students do several authentic tasks during the year. During first semester, they are required to produce a children's book—either on paper or online—or a video to teach a psychology concept to a younger child. For example, they can produce an interactive book to teach preschoolers about the five senses or a more involved story (think Magic School Bus) to introduce middle school students to the brain or nervous system. The students take the work of communicating their knowledge to younger students very seriously, and their products are thoughtful and creative.

Daniel Yong and Gabriel Lee decided to produce a "Write My Life" video tour of a Brain Museum (group interview, January 17, 2016). In the video, called *My Brain Adventure*, two hosts named Corpus and Callosum walk the viewer through various parts of the brain and their functions. The first stop is the brain stem, where Daniel and Gabriel, as the narrators, offer a playful introduction, while drawing simple pictures on a whiteboard. (The video is available at https://www.youtube.com/watch?v=e4EO0TUF41A.)

"What do you think the brain stem does?"

"Brain stem? Is that like, where the brain grows, how plants do from a plant stem?"

"You have the right idea. The brain stem is sort of where your brain grows from the spine. It controls your automatic survival functions—"

"Really? What kind of survival functions? Like how to make fire and build shelter?"

"Not that kind of survival!"

The video is accurate, funny, and engaging. It's as good as anything produced by Crash Course, and I've shared it with my students and passed it on for other teachers to use. Daniel and Gabriel said they spent about six and a half hours on the project, from 7:30 p.m. to 2:00 a.m. one night. They wanted to make it really good, and they loved the creative process, as well as knowing they were making something for an audience. "It takes time to be able to come up with a project idea and actually finish it," says Daniel. "When I'm having fun with a project, I tend to lose track of time. As a result, the hours just go by."

AP Psych students also conduct limited-scale experiments, where they do a review of the literature, propose a hypothesis, conduct tests with an experimental and control group, and present the results. One group decided to investigate whether third graders are more likely to believe someone wearing a lab coat than to believe someone dressed in casual clothing. They worked with a local elementary school and went out to teach a science lesson on clouds. They intentionally told the children false information, including that clouds are made of cotton balls. The results: they found out the kids believed whatever they were told, no matter how the "teacher" was dressed and no matter how ridiculous the information. They later debriefed the teacher and the participating children—sharing what they have learned is also part of the assignment.

HOW DO YOU INCLUDE AUTHENTIC TASKS IN YOUR INSTRUCTION?

"What are we doing? Why do we need to learn this?"

High school students demand relevance—they check out if they don't see the point of what they're learning—and there's no better way to provide it than by giving them authentic tasks.

The first step in designing an authentic task is very much like Grant Wiggins's (2009) backward design process. We need to consider the goal:

What do I want students to know? What do I want them to be able to do?
Then add: *Why is this important for them to know?*

If there's real-world applicability, then there's probably an authentic task in there somewhere.

Why do we want students to learn how to write well? I can think of many reasons beyond the college essay and academic writing. They'll need to write in many jobs, whether they are supervisors writing employee reviews and staff manuals, contractors writing bids, lawyers writing briefs, marketers writing surveys, real estate agents writing home descriptions, and so on. They'll also need to write in order to engage in public life—letters to their representatives, letters to the editor; even compelling social media posts or blogs require writing skill. And of course, they'll need to be able to write if they want their complaints to be taken seriously. I spent hours once writing a letter to the Kansas State Insurance Commissioner—a letter that ultimately got me a sizable payout from an unhelpful insurance company. Skilled writers definitely have advantages in the real world.

Wiggins wrote an entertaining piece in the *English Journal* in 2009, using results from an informal survey of friends about the kinds of writing they did at work. They listed marketing plans, memos, case histories, blogs, user manuals, legal briefs, and funding proposals. All of these could be used as authentic tasks in writing classes.

We could do the same exercise with math, science, history, economics, or public speaking—or almost any high school subject. The public policy project grew out of this thought process. The primary reason for teaching government or civics at all is to empower our students to become active, engaged citizens. If it's important for adult citizens to know how to gather information on an issue, circulate a legally acceptable petition, contact a representative, speak at a public meeting, or even run for office, then it's important for high school students to learn those skills—by using them. Far more important than memorizing facts about the structure of government.

There are a number of different ways to incorporate authentic tasks into our schools. One is to use specific projects, like the public policy project, the children's books, or student-designed experiments. These tasks aren't necessarily the everyday work of a class, but they give students an opportunity to apply what they're learning in a real-world context at various points in a class. Students typically have some class time to initiate these projects, then collaborate with classmates outside of school.

Friberg and Nippert (personal interviews, September 14, 2016) assign their biology students an authentic task related to wolf and moose populations on Isle Royale in Lake Superior. The students read a *National Geo-*

graphic article, watch a video about the ecosystem produced by scientists at Michigan Tech, and conduct a data analysis on the wolf and moose populations. They find that the population of wolves dropped from twenty-four in 2009 to just nine by February 2014, an alarming decline. Finally, they decide how they think scientists should manage the population—for example, *should humans introduce new wolves onto the island?*—and write letters to the research scientists at Michigan Tech.

Some students favor introducing new wolves:

> *Dear Mr. Vucetich and Mr. Peterson,*
>
> *The addition of new wolves to the Isle Royale wolves is vital to the survival of the wolves, and the island. Inbreeding depression has taken hold of these wolves by the throat, and only we can help. Adding new genes to the already existing wolves will help lessen inbreeding depression and increase a healthy wolf population once again.*

Others are firmly opposed:

> *Dear Mr. Vucetich and Mr. Peterson,*
>
> *I believe that humans should not introduce new wolves onto the island at all. If you did not put land wolves on the island, the island wolves will probably die out if an ice bridge is not formed. The moose population would then grow until a new predator came.*

"[Students] like it because they get to express their judgment on a situation after having a debate and analyzing the biology," Friberg says. "Knowing their thoughts and opinions will be read by someone else makes them want to put their best foot forward."

Another way to incorporate authentic tasks is to make a task, or project, the entire focus of a course. Lampert's Honors Research course is one example. Similarly, producing the *Viewer* is a course at my school, called Newspaper Production. Every day during fourth hour, students work on producing their own twelve-page newspaper, from developing story ideas to editing, copy-editing, writing headlines, taking photos, soliciting ads, creating graphics, designing pages, and sending the finished product to print.

The teacher's job—my job until this year, when I handed it off to English teacher David Ostrom—is to provide guidance (especially on tough legal or ethical issues), answer questions, manage the budget, and suggest edits to stories, while leaving most of the actual editing and production to kids. Once every two weeks or so, when the issue is about to go to print, students stay late after school for print night. Watching them work isn't so different from watching professional journalists work; there's a lot of joking and camaraderie mixed in with serious questions.

On one print night in January, students are wandering in and out of the room, shouting out questions, teasing Ostrom, occasionally crowding around one computer to discuss a thorny problem. The sun is down, but they're in no hurry to leave (classroom observation, January 17, 2017).

Daniel Yong looks up from his computer, where he is making a month-by-month time line of the crisis in Aleppo and asks, "Why is September such a long month?"

Amber Zhao answers, "You can use an abbreviation."

Daniel says, "I don't want to do that, though. It ruins the continuity."

Amber laughs. "Are you crying? Don't cry."

Daniel starts laughing in response. "I hate the month of September." A little later, he adds, "I hate November."

Then Amber, who is the managing editor, becomes engrossed in a debate over how to write a headline for pro/con editorials on teacher tenure.

"Why don't you just say, 'Is tenure beneficial? Is tenure a societal benefit?'" Amber suggests. "Then you could say on the left half, 'Tenure protects teachers' jobs' and on the right half you could say—"

"Threatens students?" Kailey Newcome, the editor in chief, suggests.

"Compromises—well, you know what I mean," Amber says.

"I kind of like 'Use' and 'Misuse,'" Ben Davis, the editorials editor, says.

"I don't really like this 'Yes and No' thing," Amber says.

They settle on a large headline: "Is Tenure Beneficial?" with two subheads: "Yes, It Secures Teachers' Jobs" and "No, It Leads to Misuse." They care about making the right word choices—they know other people will read their work, so it matters.

At some schools, journalism isn't just a one-hour-a-day class, but a massive program offering opportunities for hundreds of students. Aaron Manfull is one of two full-time journalism teachers at Francis Howell North High School in St. Charles, Missouri, and he oversees two student websites, social media, the newspaper, the photography staff, and the video program (personal interview, June 16, 2016). "I consider myself kind of in a coach position, where I'm there guiding them and working with them to practice stuff, and they're going out and playing the game," he says.

Other schools offer courses in entrepreneurship, culinary skills (that involve actual catering), and app development, which provide time for students to work on authentic projects during the school day.

Authentic tasks can also be implemented as extracurricular activities. I have about thirty students each year creating their own businesses (including SaySew) through the Junior Achievement Company Program (https://www.juniorachievement.org), which also provides mentoring by local entrepreneurs and the chance to participate in trade shows and presentation competitions (at local and national levels). The mentor and I meet with them once a week after school in the fall, then once or twice a month until we get close to the spring competitions. During the meetings, we brainstorm ideas, talk about leadership and communication, practice pitching ideas, and troubleshoot. Once the students have developed an idea, gotten product approval from JA, and set up their bank accounts, they run with their ideas on their own. (See SaySew's business report in Appendix B, Chapter 8, Sample 3, available online at sten.pub/beatboredom.)

Although it's not a class, Nandini said running a JA Company helps her draw meaning from her other classes. "It's a really good way to integrate all my subjects into one activity—design, math, how people work, and the psychology of marketing," she said. (See Figures 8.1, 8.2, and 8.3.)

WHAT ARE THE CHALLENGES OF USING AUTHENTIC TASKS?

Giving students this kind of autonomy is difficult, not because the students can't shoulder the responsibility—but because *we think they can't*. And that lack of confidence goes well beyond teachers. I can't tell you how many times I've gotten phone calls from someone in central administration that started out with "Your student called me . . ." and ended with a well-intentioned adult asking me to intercede. Some adults don't trust students with information, so they would prefer the students not ask questions. I've actually had school board members e-mail me to ask me not to let students working on public policy projects contact them because they were getting too many phone calls! That makes for an interesting, real-life lesson in citizenship. When my JA group wanted to develop the bus-tracking app, they hoped to sell it to our school district. Rather than just tell them no, a district administrator called me to ask the students to stop asking. It's frustrating. When student journalists ask questions that adults don't want to answer, once again they often ask the adviser to intervene.

Figure 8.1
Amy Helgeson, Sam Lerdahl, David Zheng, Jeman Park, and Jacob Weightman, representing Rhidian Tech, introduce themselves to the judges before their team presentation at Junior Achievement's 2016 National Student Leadership Summit.

What's worked for me (and reduced this problem, if not eliminated it completely) is to develop relationships with these individuals—central district administrators, school board members, the principal—so that usually they trust me to give the students an appropriate level of guidance. I've attended school board meetings and worked to promote positive publicity in local media around these projects, so that school administrators end up "owning" the projects and feeling proud of them, rather than irritated. Quality work also matters. It's harder (though not impossible) for administrators to censor a newspaper that's won state and national recognition, so, for example, being named finalists for the National Scholastic Press Association's Pacemaker Awards—twice—also helped.

Figure 8.2
Shelley Wang and Maddie Wang, representing Leozarb, watch as other student companies make their presentations to judges at Junior Achievement's 2016 National Student Leadership Summit.

Figure 8.3
Sam Lerdahl, Jacob Weightman, David Zheng, and Jeman Park show Senator Al Franken their Rhidian Tech scheduling app during the trade show segment of Junior Achievement's 2016 National Student Leadership Summit.

It's also important to teach students to manage conflicts and controversies in a productive way, like Anna Brockway pointed out. When my students wanted to write editorials challenging school policy, I helped them figure out how to advocate for their opinion without demeaning those who disagree or making ad hominem attacks. Focus on the goal—for example, bathroom access for transgender students—rather than on the people who might disagree, or even people who might have given them opaque answers.

The biggest challenge, of course, is when authentic tasks lead to real-world conflicts, like the prior review battle or the dissent that fractured one of my JA Companies. I'll be honest—I didn't enjoy either of those experiences; I get stressed out by conflict. But I don't want my students to become conflict avoiders or passive citizens. I want them to be assertive and confident; I want them to be leaders in our society. (I have a Far Side cartoon outside my door, with a flock of sheep listening to another sheep telling them, "Wait! Wait! Listen to me! . . . We don't HAVE to be just sheep!") If that's my philosophy, figuring out how to guide students through icky situations is part of the deal. And every year, I learn ways to do it better. This year, JA students have agreed to a bylaw that no individual owns intellectual property rights to their ideas, which should alleviate that issue, at least.

Even if we trust our students to handle this responsibility, we might wonder whether they are capable. Can students actually write publishable stories? Can they actually run businesses or conduct viable research, if we don't do it for them? I believe they can. Not every story is publishable, but many are, and students learn to edit and help each other improve their writing. (Students are actually really good at identifying when other kids plagiarize, too.) Not every page will look professional, but students like Josh Jones will discover their niche and polish the final product. Sadly, some of my graduates who have gone on to work at their college newspapers have found that other high school journalists had their page design done by advisers. What kind of message does that send?

Not every business will succeed, and not every student will complete their research endeavor either, but most students do rise to the occasion when we trust them to do real work.

Another challenge is identifying authentic tasks that fit the prescribed curriculum. In some cases, like teaching writing, science, government, and business, this is relatively straightforward. In math, it might be more challenging, since much of high school math involves building abstract concepts for higher levels of math. Still, there is so much real work to be done with math, especially with the core concepts we want students to understand, like developing number sense, understanding functions, and using equations. Students can use math skills to analyze school or state budget data and make recommendations about how the money could be better allocated. They can analyze crime patterns or traffic statistics or bus routes and, again, voice their opinions on the results to local authorities. They can conduct surveys on important community issues—such as, should the community provide open gym space for children after school?—and use statistical analysis to present the data to governing bodies. Computer science—creating apps and websites—is also full of opportunities for authentic tasks.

Another challenge is finding the resources—time, energy, and money. Students' engagement in authentic tasks can be so intense that they want to work all the time, and we just can't do that. It's not realistic to expect every teacher to work until 1:00 a.m. with students on a research project, and it can be exhausting when students keep tweaking the wording of an editorial at 7:00 p.m. on Monday, when you're just ready to send the paper to the printer and go home.

When students are working on authentic tasks, it's key that we learn to delegate. Teachers need to offer support and guidance, but we need to let go of being involved in every step. I trained my student editors to do the editing—and that's why Katrina was editing stories on her phone at the mall, and why Sisi found us a new printer without involving me. I also train student business leaders to be leaders; I expect them to communicate with each other and hold meetings outside of our regular meetings. I expect them to shoulder most of the work, which makes it manageable for me.

Financial resources are another issue; not everyone can afford a state-of-the-art classroom or even a small computer lab, like our *Viewer* newspaper office, with its eight slow desktop computers, four laptops, and five Chromebooks. The answer to that is finding grant funding, which takes effort. I've gone to local sponsor groups multiple times to get funding for new computers, new software, new cameras. When I started in 1999, I had four computers and an old copy of Pagemaker, and the computers were crowded in the back of my classroom (behind thirty-six traditional desks). Mike Lampert said he's probably raised a half million dollars in outside grant funding to provide his students with all of the resources they need. Almost no teacher has the money they need, but it's out there. Some authentic tasks, like the public policy project, require nothing more than access to computers in a lab or library.

A final barrier to using authentic tasks is the fear that they won't teach the kinds of content tested on state-mandated tests or college entrance exams. Setting aside the issue of whether those are the best measures of student learning, research has shown that students whose teachers embrace authentic instruction do perform better, even on multiple-choice content tests. The lack of lecture and repetition is more than made up for by the students' deep engagement in their tasks. The key is for us to guide students toward appropriate, challenging tasks that require students to learn what we want them to know.

TIPS FOR TEACHERS

How do I get started if I have never used authentic tasks?

- Start with backward design. What do I want students to know? What do I want them to be able to do? Why is this important for them to know? Think about how the concepts and skills in your curriculum relate to civic participation, understanding of world affairs, consumer competency, or job skills, and develop a task that requires students to do real-world work.

- Start simple, with a moderate task like writing letters to the editor (or to researchers in a particular field) or conducting a survey on a local government issue.

- Set clear parameters, then give students the freedom to do work they care about. Be clear about what is acceptable—for example, I let the student journalists editorialize in favor of marijuana legalization, but not in favor of illegal marijuana use. I wouldn't let them start a business that might put other students at risk, like a Craigslist-style app.

- Give students examples of the kinds of work other students are doing. Many school newspapers, businesses, and research competitions have websites that can serve as exemplars.

How can I build on my use of authentic tasks to encourage better participation and deeper learning?

- As you grow more confident in helping students develop their own authentic tasks, the key is to listen and trust them. I frequently find my internal voice saying, "That's a terrible idea" when JA students propose a new venture, but I don't say that out loud. Who am I to quash their creative ideas? (I probably would have told Apple never to make iPhones—that's how good my business sense is.) The same can be applied to scientific research, public policy projects, and newspaper stories. Let students pursue their own ideas, and they'll be much more deeply invested, even if they turn out to be wrong.

- Encourage larger-scale projects, even semesterlong projects, new extracurricular clubs, or new courses. Show your administrators what other schools are doing, and let them see the kinds of student engagement, positive publicity, and good outcomes they generate.

- Focus on getting disadvantaged students involved. That's the benefit of incorporating authentic tasks in the classroom setting; then they are not reserved for students who have time to pursue extracurriculars or independent projects.

How will I assess and know if it's effective?

- Develop rubrics for assessing student work on assignments like the public policy project or independent research, where every student group will produce different final products. Using checkpoints or project steps is helpful. On the public policy project, my students were required to turn in four steps: (1) A description of the problem, including evidence of the problem and potential causes; (2) a list of alternative policy choices, including their favored solution; (3) an action plan for civic involvement; and (4) a presentation that included a report on their personal action steps.

- Use contracts to set clear expectations when students are working in a group production setting. My news editors agreed to contracts outlining the expectations for their jobs at the beginning of each year, and they turned in self-assessments of how well they were performing their duties before I evaluated each issue. This minimized conflict over issues like deadlines and editing expectations.

- Use the same assessments of course objectives. If you are using an authentic task to teach the scientific process or writing skills, students can still be expected to show their knowledge on conventional assessments.

AFTERWORD

When I began my student teaching as an assignment for the *Wichita Eagle* in 1993, my goal was to become a better education reporter, with more insight into what really happens in schools. I never expected to actually become a high school teacher, and I never dreamed I would still be teaching nearly twenty-five years later.

I kept a journal of my student-teaching experience, and the *Eagle* published it in two installments in early 1994 with the headline, "What I Learned: A Student Teacher's Story."

It's a little embarrassing now to reread those journal entries. I thought I had learned so much, as an "insider" to the school system. I thought I knew something about being an effective teacher after just eight weeks in middle school and eight weeks in high school, all with cooperating teachers holding my hand.

It's useful to reread the journals, though, to remind me what it was like to be a brand-new teacher—what I was afraid of, what I was excited about, what I wanted for my classroom, and what made the days good or, in some cases, unbearable.

I wrote about struggling to be creative, being surprised to feel like an authority figure, stumbling while trying to initiate discussions, finding joy when a student actually made a connection, and enjoying the feeling of expertise when a lecture went well.

Here are a few excerpts:

> *Aug. 23, 1993—I've read countless books and*
> *essays that preach creativity in everything from*
> *testing to seating arrangements. But how do you just*

*walk into a classroom and be creative? Like most
people, I went to traditional public schools, where
the teacher lectured and the students did homework
and took tests. For all that I've heard and read, I
still don't see how to do it any other way. I have no
idea what kind of teacher I'll be.*

*Aug. 27, 1993—I had feared I would not feel like a
real teacher, but once the students were there, I was
struck by a sudden sense of my own authority.*

*Aug. 30, 1993—As calmly as I could, I took
attendance, passed out books, tried to start a
discussion. What is "civics"? I asked them. What
are rights? No answers. I asked about current
events. No takers. First hour seemed to last a week.*

*Aug. 31, 1993—Almost all of the kids did their
homework—they did what I said! It's weird to have
that power.*

*Sept. 14, 1993—They really struggled on the
multiple choice and fill-in-the-blank parts [of a
test]. The essays were good, though. All but two kids
argued vehemently against raising the driving age.
One said: "Parents are too old and need their kids
to drive them around." One said he would make his
point by recruiting thousands of teenagers to drive
to Topeka and around the Capitol. I love it.*

Oct. 1, 1993—In first hour, we had an incredibly raucous debate about the city's proposed quarter-cent sales tax to fight crime. I planted the discord by giving half the class a pro-sales-tax article to read and half the class an anti-tax article. Two girls just about ended up in a fight. . . . Students in my later classes asked if they could do "that debate." How can I even explain how good it feels to get kids that passionate about something? I wanted to videotape them, to somehow save that moment to remind me on days when nothing goes right. Thank you, girls.

Oct. 28, 1993—I flopped in P's classes. When he stepped out, the kids went wild. When he returned, they immediately calmed down. One of the kids said, "Notice how everyone's quiet now?" P chastised them. I felt lame for not doing something myself.

Nov. 1, 1993—I did much better in P's class today. I tried to be as much like him as possible, lecturing in a no-nonsense voice and refusing to tolerate talking. This is not my style at all, but it went well.

Nov. 9, 1993—The US History I Honors class is going to act out the Constitutional Convention. . . . I have nothing creative or special planned for the US History I regular class. Not enough kids show up to pull off this kind of activity. In addition, it would take more independent work than I think they're willing to do. They probably need creative teaching more than anyone, but I'm at a loss.

*Dec. 6, 1993—I had such a fantastic time with
the US History II class today that I did not want
it to end. I think it was the first time I really felt
qualified to teach those kids, many of whom are at
college level. I was lecturing on business practices
in the 1920s, stock market speculation, and what
caused the 1929 crash. As usual, they questioned
everything. But for the first time, I knew all the
answers. I told them how the stock market works,
why companies sell stock, how orders are placed,
why prices go up and down, why buying on the
margin can hurt people. . . . At Newman, the
professors discouraged lecturing. I'm not wedded to
it myself—I think kids learn more by finding things
out for themselves than they do by having a teacher
stand in front of them and dispense information. But
boy, it feels good when it works.*

When I reread these journals, here's what stands out to me: I was young,
naïve, and very optimistic. I wanted so badly to do a good job, to be creative,
to deeply engage my students. I had read every popular book and news report
on effective teaching published between 1991 and 1993, and visited probably
one hundred classrooms in my time as an education reporter, so I knew what
I wanted my own teaching experience to be like.

Still, many forces were already luring me back to the traditional, lecture-
oriented path, and I quickly gave up on active learning strategies when the
going got tough. I didn't even try the simulation with the regular history class.

Why did I let this happen? Why didn't I follow my convictions? Why did
I end up lecturing so much, and liking it? For a few reasons, I think.

Two of my three cooperating teachers were very traditional: no talking,
no late work, no group work, no excuses. Desks were lined up in rigid rows,
and everything was teacher directed. (Bill Jenkins, whom I describe in my
journal as a '60s holdover, was the exception. He's the one who gave me
the World War I hearing simulation.) It was easier most days to teach the
way my colleagues taught, and when my more adventurous ideas failed, they
were quick to steer me back to a more cautious approach. *You can't let them*

get away with anything, they would tell me. Or, *These kids aren't very good at discussing.*

On top of that, the students were well trained in traditional schooling. They would sit quietly and seem to listen if I lectured in a "no-nonsense" style, but they "went wild" when I gave them any leeway. Although I was able to stir some discussion (the sales tax debate) and successfully implement a simulation (the Constitutional Convention), I also ran into times when those strategies just didn't seem to work, when it was easier to revert to the teacher-centered comfort zone. And when the kids didn't do well on tests, that was a wakeup call. I felt like I had to do what my cooperating teachers suggested; I didn't have the confidence to do it differently.

Perhaps most important, being in charge felt good. It was weirdly invigorating. I was amazed over and over when students listened to me, when they followed my instructions, when they did homework, when they seemed interested in what I was saying. There's no question that being the center of students' attention was an ego boost.

I think my experience captures what a lot of teachers go through in our careers. We face a constant tension between wanting to be creative, wanting to try active-learning strategies, wanting to do things differently—and yet feeling more comfortable and in control in a traditional lecture-style classroom. In some cases, that feeling is reinforced by peers or administrators who actively discourage us from using nontraditional strategies. "I have come to loggerheads with my administration many times," Mike Lampert told me (personal interview, June 16, 2016).

Doing things differently is hard.

The bottom line is this: no one becomes a teacher so they can bore kids. But traditional lecture-and-memorize instruction is part of our culture. It's deeply ingrained, it's easier than any alternative, and it's hard to change by yourself. Students even seem to prefer it, because it doesn't ask much of them. It lets them get away with zoning out.

But this kind of instruction does not deeply engage high school students, and it's not the most effective way to teach them.

When I started working on this book, I surveyed hundreds of recent graduates on their experiences in high school. One thing I wanted to know was, *When you were highly engaged in class, what was the class doing?* I thought I knew what the answers would be, based on my own observations and conversations with my students, but I wanted to see what an anonymous group of students—not connected to me, not trying to please me—would say.

Here are a few of their responses:

- *Students were allowed an opportunity to share their ideas.*

- *Learning about real-life situations.*

- *We were all talking; we were all putting in our opinions or trying to guess what would happen next (in a book we were reading).*

- *Doing hands-on activities.*

- *My government class, the teacher made us debate. He was a student just like everyone else; we took control over the class as students (I was the president).*

- *Having a class discussion over a controversial topic in a foreign language, in order to improve our speaking skills.*

- *Not having to participate by taking notes, but learning by doing.*

A few mentioned listening to a good lecture, but not many. Only seven students—1 percent of those surveyed—said their teachers were all excellent lecturers.

I also asked the graduates to recommend their most engaging teacher. That's how I found several of the teachers I interviewed, and I soon discovered that these teachers were using the same kinds of active-learning strategies I've been using. This kind of instruction resonates with their students.

"Seeing how [the STEM program] works and the way that teachers work with students motivated me to switch from wanting to be an engineer to wanting to be a teacher. That's been a huge change. It's kind of like passing it forward or giving it back, the impact STEM has had on me, I want to give back to the students," said Marco Garcia (personal interview, February 23, 2017), one of the students in José Garcia's STEM program.

I know active learning resonates with my students, too. When I talk with my former students, they talk about how they felt engaged, empowered, interested, and excited about learning. They talk about how their classes in civil liberties or economics or psychology or journalism shaped their thought processes, their career goals, and even their lives.

"I feel like Civil Liberties was the first place in school where there was a space for us, as a class, to have actual discussions about specific issues that provided some more nuance," Anna Brockway told me (personal interview, February 28, 2016).

"Having the opportunity to reflect on such an important experience as part of a class was pretty cool and definitely something I hadn't done before in school," said Ryan Yoch, reflecting on his "Defining Moment" essay (personal interview, November 24, 2016). "It made me realize how grateful I was for my friends and how far I'd come since being bullied in middle school."

"It boils down to I'm an economics major today mainly because of doing competitions," said Sola Olateju (personal interview, October 26, 2016). "It's a very different teaching style, not in any other classes I'd had before that."

Engaging students with active-learning strategies can have a profound effect. It can change kids' minds about school, open doors to civic engagement and career opportunities, overcome barriers to learning, and close the gap between privileged and disadvantaged students. It won't always make students obey or sit still or listen, but it can make them excited about school, even when they have almost given up, and it can even inspire them to want to teach others. I feel fortunate that I have had the freedom and ability to engage in this kind of teaching with so many fantastic, capable students.

When I was a student teacher nearly twenty-five years ago, I discovered that using active learning and living up to my ideals about teaching was not easy. In the intervening years, I've learned that it's definitely worth the effort.

APPENDIX

For additional materials, including academic research and additional student samples, please visit sten.pub/beatboredom.

CHAPTER 3, SAMPLE 1

Defining Moment
by Ryan Yoch

I was standing nervously in my tiny blue gym shorts and my baggy red gym shirt when one of the prettiest girls I had ever seen taught me how to hug.

"You suck at hugging," she laughed as I tried to stick my hands in my pocketless gym shorts.

"We didn't really give hugs at my old school," I told her.

"Well, we do here. Here, I'll teach you," she smiled. I opened my chapped lips to protest, but it was too late. "Okay, even though I'm taller than you, you are going to want to put your arms on the inside, okay? Okay. And . . . relax," she smiled as she moved in for try #2.

This one went much better. My arms were in the right spots and I was a lot less tense. I thanked her and tried to scurry away, but she wasn't going to let me go that easily. "Hey Ryan," she called after me.

"Yeah?"

"Can we be best friends?" she asked with her powerful smile.

"Uhh . . . yeah," I mumbled. I may not have seemed excited, but for the rest of my first week at Chippewa, and the rest of my 7th grade year, I couldn't stop thinking about her. Katie Tschida, my first real friend.

You have to understand . . . this was a big deal for me. I was miserable at my old school. They used to make me sit by myself at lunch. They used to invite all 41 kids in our grade except me to parties and then talk about how much fun they had at school. They used to make me feel like I didn't belong.

That was why I switched schools. I couldn't take coming home from school every day and crying because all I really wanted was a friend. And my parents couldn't take it either. The decision to pull me from my private school and throw me into the public, Chippewa Middle School, was terrifying.

I remember the night before the first day of school. It was 3 in the morning and I was wide awake. I went outside, by myself, to sit on our porch. I couldn't stop crying. The kids at my previous school had destroyed me inside and out. So much so that I thought there was something wrong with ME. That I was the weird one. That I would never amount to anything. That I would never make a friend.

But the decision to move me to Chippewa was the best decision my parents and I have ever made. By the end of the year, I couldn't stop smiling. I had friends! SO MANY FRIENDS! And they loved me. Even though my voice was high and my face was round, they loved me.

The switch to Chippewa made me who I am today. Confident in myself, trusting of others . . . and most importantly of all, happy.

CHAPTER 3, SAMPLE 2

Defining Moment
by Maddy Rosenow

It was here. The day had finally come. It was my first practice of traveling basketball. The whole day my stomach had been churning in anticipation, and my thoughts racing with what practice would consist of.

I couldn't do my homework after school, my focus was elsewhere. I was counting down the hours until six o'clock. My mom made me a typical elementary-schooler dinner, consisting of two corn dogs and a heaping portion of Mac and Cheese. My two favorite foods at the time, both of which I now find repulsive. I vividly remember scarfing the nutritious meal down, thinking I needed to have the most energy out there.

As the time came to leave for practice, I couldn't have thrown my spanking new practice jersey on fast enough. I grabbed my new, pink of course, Nike drawstring and rushed out the door. My practice was at Chippewa, I was in the big gyms now. No more of the small slippery cafeteria "gyms" I was used to.

As I leaped out of the car and slammed the car door, more thoughts raced into my mind. I thought about my new teammates. I had a couple good friends on the team, one of them was Nancy*. Her dad was the coach. I had met him a couple times at her house. He seemed nice, but had really broad shoulders. The fact that he was partly bald really intimidated me. He had this booming voice too, it just wanted to make you shrink down into a ball. Little did I know that a basketball court provided really good acoustics for that booming voice.

As I walked into the school, cradling my shiny new white and blue Adidas, the butterflies in my stomach were really fluttering. I knew that if anyone looked at me at that moment, they would see a beaming smile on my face, and visible pride in being a basketball player.

Unsurprisingly, I was the first one there. I sat down against the blue matted wall and laced up my shoes. I stood up and looked down at my new prized possessions. I sauntered over to the ball rack and grabbed ahold of the shiny Spalding at the top. A few more girls poked their heads in the gym, recognized me, and filed in.

I bounced my ball once and walked slowly onto the court. I stood at the block and shot some layups, I was too scared to go any farther. My audience of teammates was making me nervous. I didn't want to be that one girl who missed an easy long shot.

As more girls showed up, the girls who knew each other started to chit chat, and it was a lively friendly atmosphere. We were all shooting, laughing, and enjoying ourselves. I remember thinking, "This is going to be a fun team."

A hush fell over the gym as broad shouldered Coach walked in. We all gathered under the basket closest to the door. "I'm your coach," he said booming. A silent moment passed. Enough time for all us girls to look at each other questioning. One of the bolder girls, Meghan, decided to fill the silence. She was always good at that. "Should we like introduce ourselves or something?" I remember thinking, "Oh dear gosh, she'll be fun."

Although Meghan's idea seemed perfectly normal for the first practice, Coach had another idea in mind.

"Get on the line, girls," he practically screamed. It was apparent that none of our previous coaches believed in the idea of killers. Rounds of "What line?" or "Which line?" went around us group of girls. "What the hell do you mean what line?" screamed Coach. "The end line of course!"

I remember being stunned that he would swear at us. I had never been sworn at before. I looked around the girls. Meghan, the bold one, was muttering swear words under her breath. We all walked, almost a crawling pace, to the end line. I took a spot next to a girl named Lexi.

As it dawned on me that we were actually going to run, one thought came streaking into my mind. "MY INHALER." I had forgotten to take it and bring it. My stomach dropped. I knew that with my asthma, running more than a couple killers was going to be really hard. Being sworn at still prevented me from speaking up about my asthma.

He gave his whistle one long defiant shriek. We took off sprinting to the free throw line and back, half back, other free throw line and back, and all the way down the other end line and back. As soon as the last girl crossed the final end line, the whistle shrieked again. The routine of down and backs repeated. The first few weren't bad, but as the whistle continued to shriek I remember thinking of the movie *Miracle on Ice*. I remembered the iconic scene with Herb Brooks blowing his whistle and repeating "AGAIN!" over and over again. Except Coach was Herb Brooks, and we were the USA hockey team.

As the killers continued we were all groaning to stop. It had to be around the tenth killer when I started to feel my lungs shrinking. I was gasping and wheezing. I was starting to regret that gourmet dinner of corn dogs and Mac and Cheese. I got to half court of whatever killer it was, quickly turned around and ran to the bathroom as fast as my shaking legs could take me. I remember making it only to the sink, and there went my dinner. Tears streaked down my face. Along with my dinner went my love for the game.

I walked out of the gym after that practice of all killers feeling defeated and humiliated. I dreaded every practice and every game that season, and every season to follow. Every day after that practice I didn't cradle my shoes, I lugged them. I didn't bound in beaming, I sulked in. I wasn't the first to practice, I was normally rushing in late. Those killers, that swear word, and that intimidating coach wrecked the game of basketball for me.

*Name has been changed.

CHAPTER 5, SAMPLE 1

Closing the Gap
by Libby Fleming

According to the Organisation for Economic Cooperation and Development, the United States ranks well behind high-performing countries in K–12 academic performance. As of 2012, the United States was ranked 27th in math and 17th in reading (*United States*). To improve student outcomes, the United States should adopt a 12-month academic year, eliminating the 12-week summer break and replacing it with more frequent, shorter breaks throughout the year. Students and teachers would have the same number of school days as the current system. This schedule would be cost-neutral and result in improved student outcomes, particularly reduced summer learning loss and higher educational attainment for at-risk students.

The majority of K–12 school systems in the United States currently follow the same schedule that was popularized in the late 1800s. This schedule consists of approximately 180 days of school scheduled over nine months, from the beginning of September to the end of May. The three-month summer break was established when agrarian life was prominent (DeNisco). "Children were in school, but not when they were needed for the work-intensive summer harvest. The nine-month school year accommodated the need" (Gilbert). Today, only three percent of Americans' lives are based on the agricultural cycle (Cooper et al). Because the United States is no longer a predominantly agrarian economy, it no longer makes economic sense to operate by this schedule.

For most American K–12 students, the summer break is a chance to unplug. Unfortunately, unplugging results in a loss of much of the material learned during the school year. Regardless of the resources at home, studies have shown that most students lose an average of one month of math skills over the summer (Cooper et al). Even worse, the loss of reading and comprehension skills is greater for students from lower income families. These disadvantaged students can lose up to three months of reading skills over the summer (Granderson). Many disadvantaged students make similar academic gains as advantaged students during the school year, but the gap widens in the summer as they face greater loss of material (Huebner). In one study comparing students from high and low socioeconomic status (SES) groups in Baltimore, researchers tested students in the spring and fall each year, starting in first grade and following the students through ninth grade. The researchers found that high SES students improved test scores from spring to fall, whereas low SES students scored more poorly in the fall (Alexander et al). This difference in what students lose is caused by unequal summer opportunities. Students without the same enrichment opportunities as advantaged students do not receive the additional learning provided by camps, organized sports, and travel (Donohue et al). The Baltimore study researchers concluded, "A large portion of the achievement gap originates over the summer, when children are not in school. The resource disparity children from lower-income families experience fuels this achievement gap growth" (Alexander et al). Without costly interventions to get them back on track, disadvantaged students lose ground and never catch up. By adopting a schedule that eliminates an extended summer break and intersperses short breaks during the year, all students would be less likely to suffer from learning loss, and disadvantaged students would be less likely to start out behind each school year.

The loss of material over the summer is so great that American K–12 teachers typically use the first month of each school year to re-teach what was lost (Granderson). The opportunity cost of the time teachers spend re-teaching is the foregone ability to teach new or deeper study of content. With a year-round school calendar, teachers would spend less time re-teaching, and they would be able to teach material they would not have otherwise had time to present (Granderson). Not only would this improve teacher productivity, it would also improve student outcomes as they would have the benefit of deeper exposure to subjects.

Moreover, by implementing a full-year school calendar, students who are at risk for dropping out may be more motivated to stay in school and graduate. With a schedule of short, frequent breaks, students are less likely to burn out and be discouraged. In addition, studies have shown that more frequent, spaced out breaks decrease the amount of student and staff absences (Weaver). Fewer absences would likely result in better student outcomes and cost savings through reduced need to cover teacher absences.

While there are a number of advocates for adoption of a year round K–12 school year, there are also critics. One economic concern is the cost of staff salaries. Some critics note that if schools are open for 12 months, teachers and staff would need to be paid 12 month salaries (Cooper et al). However, teachers would be teaching for the same amount of days, so their overall salaries would not necessarily change. Another concern is from students who need income of their own. A long summer vacation provides an opportunity for students to earn money that can be put toward their future college education or living expenses. Advocates for 12-month school calendars say that employers could adopt job-sharing arrangements, where students would work during their school break and return at their next break (Cooper et al).

It may take more creative scheduling and flexibility, but there are ways for students to earn income with a 12-month school calendar.

The American K–12 education system needs to better prepare students to compete globally. The issues are complex and there is no one solution; however, the United States must take bold action to improve its education system. Adopting a year round calendar is a cost effective solution to improving student outcomes. It may not be the most popular change, but it offers strong potential for student improvement without increasing per student spending.

WORKS CITED

Alexander, K. L., D. R. Entwisle, and L. S. Olson. "Lasting Consequences of the Summer Learning Gap." *American Sociological Review* 72.2 (2007): 167–80. Web. 15 Mar. 2016.

Alexander, K. L., D. R. Entwisle, and L. S. Olson. "Summer Learning and Its Implications: Insights from the Beginning School Study." *New Directions for Youth Development* 2007.114 (2007): 11–32. *EBSCO MegaFILE*. Web. 15 Mar. 2016.

Cooper, Harris, et al. "The Effects of Modified School Calendars on Student Achievement and on School and Community Attitudes." *Review of Educational Research* 73.1 (2003): 1–52. *ProQuest*. Web. 28 Feb. 2016.

DeNisco, Alison. "Year-Round Schooling Gains Popularity." *District Administration* 51.9 (2015): 16–18. *Academic Search Premier.* Web. 28 Feb. 2016.

Donohue, Nicholas C., and Beth M. Miller. "Stemming Summer Learning Loss." *The New England Journal of Higher Education.* ProQuest Educational Journals, 2008. Web. 14 Mar. 2016.

Gilbert, Michael. "A Plea for Systemic Change in Education." *On the Horizon* 21.4 (2013): 312–22. *ProQuest.* Web. 23 Mar. 2016.

Granderson, LZ. "We Need Year-Round School to Compete Globally." CNN. Cable News Network, 11 May 2011. Web. 28 Feb. 2016.

Huebner, Tracy A. "Year-Round Schooling." *Educational Leadership* 67.7 (2010): 83–84. *Academic Search Premier.* Web. 28 Feb. 2016.

"United States." *OECD.* N.p., n.d. Web. 28 Feb. 2016.

Weaver, Tyler. "Year-Round Education." *Year-Round Education. ERIC Digest.* N.p., n.d. Web. 28 Feb. 2016.

CHAPTER 8, SAMPLE 1

"Significant arrest" raises questions about MV drug use
by Anna Brockway
Editor in chief
(published Dec. 21, 2007)

A 16-year-old male was arrested for possession and intent to sell drugs on school property on Monday, Nov. 12. The arrest followed the search of a vehicle in the school parking lot, according to the Ramsey County Sheriff Department's incident report.

According to the police report, the vehicle contained suspected marijuana, suspected cocaine, suspected mushrooms, 9 pills of suspected Ecstasy, 1 digital scale, and $265.

The substances later tested positive for 6.6g of Cocaine HCL, trace amounts of crack cocaine, and 47g of marijuana. The presence of MDMA, a psychoactive drug commonly sold in the form of Ecstasy tablets, was confirmed in the pills. The testing time on the 23g of mushrooms was longer than allowed for the publication of the supplementary report.

Steve Robertson, Special Agent with the U.S. Drug Enforcement Administration, said that the variety of drugs, more so than the amount, was "the sign for a very sophisticated drug operation."

He continued, "Based on my experience throughout the nation, that's a pretty significant arrest."

School officials could not comment on the incident, but they stressed that drugs are not unfamiliar to Mounds View.

"Typically, I will petition or charge out 4–6 [students] a school year—that includes drugs and alcohol," said School Resource Officer Glen Pothen.

While students have been arrested in the past for possession and use, members of the administration stressed that for as long as they'd been here, no cases had matched this incident in magnitude.

"It's news because it's unusual; it attracts people's attention," said Principal Julie Wikelius.

"When you're talking about schools, you're typically talking about small amounts. To that degree, this situation was unique to Mounds View and probably most schools," said Dean Paul Anderson. "Mounds View struggles with the same social ills as any other school within this state, city and country. I don't think any realistic adult or student ever thought that Mounds View was a drug-free environment."

Since the individual was arrested with intent to sell, the question arose if the arrest could lead to charges of buyers in the school community. The administration declined to comment.

However, the arrest of a dealer could leave a provider vacancy in the underground substance-use community. In cases such as this one, Pothen said, the rebound time is unclear.

"It can vary—we see a lot of times where it's a very short time before the hole has been filled, so to speak, and other times when it never has," he said.

Drug users within Mounds View, who agreed to speak to the *Viewer* on condition of anonymity, are worried about the availability and reliability of harder substances in light of this arrest. A concern for users is that they don't always know what they're getting. Trust is an issue between users and providers, as drugs such as Ecstasy often come laced with other, more dangerous, substances.

"It's not like other districts drug dealers—there's only a few people so it's difficult to know who to trust," said Jill, 12, whose name has been changed.

However, Pothen and Anderson both said that the prevalence of drugs within MV is comparable to that of nearby high schools such as Irondale, Roseville, and White Bear Lake.

"I think it's very similar to other schools," said Anderson. "[However], I think schools handle this issue very differently. I think Mounds View does an excellent job in this area."

According to the Minnesota Student Survey, led by the Department of Education and administered in the spring of 2004 for 6th, 9th and 12th graders, 17 percent of 9th grade boys and 18 percent of 9th grade girls had used both alcohol and drugs (excluding tobacco) in the past year. The numbers rose to 30 percent of boys and 25 percent of girls for students in 12th grade. The survey was administered again in the spring of 2007, but results were not yet available at the time of this publication.

This anonymous survey is relied on by administrators to give accurate assessments of the frequency of drugs and alcohol within their school communities.

"Certainly, that number [reporting alcohol and drug use] was larger than any of us would like it to be," said Wikelius.

Staff and faculty do not specifically monitor students for drug use, but that doesn't mean the school is unaware.

"I and others have worked and trained staff for what to look for in students who are under the influence of drugs and chemicals," said Anderson.

In the past, the school community has taken other measures to counter substance abuse. Alco-blows were implemented at MV dances in the fall of

2006; green open-door policy posters were placed inside every classroom by the school-sponsored Students Against Destructive Decision-making (SADD) in the spring of 2006; and Minnesota State High School League activity substance rules are strictly enforced within the school.

"I think what does help Mounds View is that all of the students here have an understanding that as staff, we have a deep, deep commitment to a safe school, and I think what occurred [reinforces] the school's commitment to our sense of responsibility," Anderson said.

"A lot of it has to do with parents keeping eyes on what's going on with [their] kids, being aware of what kids are doing and being responsible parents," said Pothen. "I think our parents are very involved with our students."

REFERENCES

Abbeduto, Leonard, and Frank Symons. 2009. *Taking Sides: Clashing Views on Controversial Issues in Educational Psychology*. New York: McGraw-Hill.

Abernathy, Tammy V., and Richard N. Vineyard. 2001. "Academic Competitions in Science." *Clearing House* 74 (May/June): 269–276. ERIC [EBSCO].

Akpinar, Murat, Cristina Del Campo, and Enes Eryarsoy. 2014. "Learning Effects of an International Group Competition Project." *Innovations in Education and Teaching International* 52 (2): 160–171. doi:10.1080/14703297.2014.880656.

Alayont, Feryal. 2014. "Using Problem-Based Pre-Class Activities to Prepare Students for In-Class Learning." *PRIMUS* 24 (2): 138–148. doi: 10.1080/10511970.2013.844510.

Applebee, Arthur N., Judith A. Langer, Martin Nystrand, and Adam Gamoran. 2003. "Discussion-Based Approaches to Developing Understanding: Classroom Instruction and Student Performance in Middle and High School English." *American Educational Research Journal* 40 (3): 685–730.

Ariely, Dan. 2010. *The Upside of Irrationality: The Unexpected Benefits of Defying Logic at Work and at Home*. New York: Harper.

Auman, Corinne. 2011. "Using Simulation Games to Increase Student and Instructor Engagement." *College Teaching* 59 (4): 154–161. doi: 10.1080/87567555.2011.602134.

Bench, Shane W., and Heather C. Lench. 2013. "On the Function of Boredom." *Behavioral Science* 3 (August 15): 459–472. doi:10.3390/bs3030459.

Benke, Gertraud. 2012. "Robotics Competitions and Science Classrooms." *Cultural Studies of Science Education* 7 (2): 416–423. doi:10.1007/s11422-012-9400-8.

Bennett, Ty. 2014. *The Power of Storytelling: The Art of Influential Communication*. American Fork, UT: Sound Concepts.

Bernstein, Jeffrey L., and Deborah S. Meizlish. 2003. "Becoming Congress: A Longitudinal Study of the Civic Engagement Implications of a Classroom Simulation." *Simulation & Gaming* 34 (2): 198–219. Doi:10.1177/10468781030340 02003.

Bernstein-Yamashiro, Beth. 2004. "Learning Relationships: Teacher-Student Connections, Learning, and Identity in High School." *New Directions for Youth Development* 103: 55–70. doi:10.1002/yd.91.

Blackmon, Stephanie J. 2012. "Outcomes of Chat and Discussion Board Use in Online Learning: A Research Synthesis." *Journal of Educators Online* 9 (2): 19.

Bridgeland, John, John DiIulio, and Karen Morison. 2006. *The Silent Epidemic: Perspectives of High School Dropouts*. Report. https://docs.gatesfoundation.org/documents/thesilentepidemic3-06final.pdf.

Bridgeland, John, Mary Bruce, and Arya Hariharan. 2013. *The Missing Piece: A National Teacher Survey on How Social and Emotional Learning Can Empower Children and Transform Schools*. A report for CASEL. http://www.civicenterprises.net/MediaLibrary/Docs/CASEL-Report-low-res-FINAL.pdf.

Brockway, Anna. 2007. "'Significant Arrest' Raises Questions About MV Drug Use." *Viewer* 54 (5): 1.

Brown, Peter C., Henry L. Roediger, and Mark A. McDaniel. 2014. *Make It Stick: The Science of Successful Learning*. Cambridge, MA: Belknap Press of Harvard University Press.

Capaldi, Nicholas. 1999. *How to Win Every Argument*. New York: MJF Books.

Carr, Nicholas G. 2010. *The Shallows: What the Internet Is Doing to Our Brains*. New York: W. W. Norton.

Chicago-Kent College of Law at Illinois Tech. 1989. "Texas v. Johnson." Oyez. https://www.oyez.org/cases/1988/88-155.

The Choices Program. 2008–2009. Providence, RI: Watson Center for International Studies, Brown University. http://www.choices.edu/resources/documents/resourcebook_09.pdf

Chorzempa, Barbara Fink, and Laurie Lapidus. 2009. "To Find Yourself, Think for Yourself." *TEACHING Exceptional Children* 41 (3): 54–59. doi:10.1177/004005990904100306.

Chowning, Jeanne T. 2009. "Socratic Seminars in Science Class: Providing a Structured Format to Promote Dialogue and Understanding." *The Science Teacher* 26 (October): 36–41. doi:130.91.116.161.

Chung, C. J. C., Christopher Cartwright, and Matthew Cole. 2014. "Assessing the Impact of an Autonomous Robotics Competition for STEM Education." *Journal of STEM Education: Innovations and Research* 15 (2): 24–34.

Corso, Michael, Matthew Bundick, Russell Quaglia, and Dawn Haywood. 2013. "Where Student, Teacher, and Content Meet: Student Engagement in the Secondary School Classroom." *American Secondary Education* 41 (3): 50–61.

Crookall, David. 2010. "Serious Games, Debriefing, and Simulation/ Gaming as a Discipline." *Simulation & Gaming* 41 (6): 898–920. doi:10.1177/1046878110390784.

———. 2014. "Engaging (in) Gameplay and (in) Debriefing." *Simulation & Gaming* 45 (4–5): 416–427. doi:10.1177/1046878114559879.

Csikszentmihalyi, Mihaly. 2009. *Flow: The Psychology of Optimal Experience*. New York: Harper Row.

Dallimore, Elise J., Julie H. Hertenstein, and Marjorie B. Platt. 2012. "Impact of Cold-Calling on Student Voluntary Participation." *Journal of Management Education* 37 (3): 305–341. doi:10.1177/1052562912446067.

Duke, Charles R. 1988. "Giving the Competitive Edge to Students' Academic Achievement." *NASSP Bulletin* 72 (507): 1–7. doi:10.1177/019263658807250702.

Eastwood, John. 2014. "What Is Boredom?" www.boredomlab.org.

Ertmer, Peggy A., Sarah Schlosser, Kari Clase, and Omolola Adedokun. 2014. "The Grand Challenge: Helping Teachers Learn/Teach Cutting-Edge Science via a PBL Approach." *Interdisciplinary Journal of Problem-Based Learning* 8 (1). doi:10.7771/1541-5015.1407.

Ertmer, Peggy A., and Krista D. Simons. 2006. "Jumping the PBL Implementation Hurdle: Supporting the Efforts of K–12 Teachers." *Interdisciplinary Journal of Problem-Based Learning* 1 (1): 40–54. doi: 10.7771/1541-5015.1005.

Fine, Sarah. "A Slow Revolution: Toward a Theory of Intellectual Playfulness in High School Classrooms." 2014. *Harvard Educational Review* 84 (1): 1–23. doi:10.17763/haer.84.1.qtr193464843n334.

Firmin, Michael W., Aaron Vaughn, and Amanda Dye. 2007. "Using Debate to Maximize Learning Potential: A Case Study." *Journal of College Teaching & Learning (TLC)* 4 (1): 19–32. doi:10.19030/

tlc.v4i1.1635.

Fisher, Douglas. 2009. "The Use of Instructional Time in the Typical High School Classroom." *The Educational Forum* 73 (2): 168–176. doi:10.1080/00131720902739650.

For Which It Stands: Flag-Burning and the First Amendment. 1992. VHS. Alexandria, VA: Close-Up.

Frank, Anne. *The Diary of a Young Girl*. New York: Pocket Books, 1990.

Fuller, Renee. 1991. "The Primacy of Story." *In Context* 27 (Winter): 26–28. ERIC [EBSCO]. https://eric.ed.gov/?q=The+Primacy+of+Story&ft=on&id=ED354691.

Gallagher, Shelagh A., and James J. Gallagher. 2013. "Using Problem-Based Learning to Explore Unseen Academic Potential." *Interdisciplinary Journal of Problem-Based Learning* 7 (1): 111–131. doi:10.7771/1541-5015.1322.

Gjedde, Lisa. 2014. "Potentials of a Narrative Game-Based Curriculum Framework for Enhancing Motivation and Collaboration." Academic Conferences International Limited, 10. http://vbn.aau.dk/en/publications/potentials-of-a-narrative-game-based-curriculum-framework-for-enhancing-motivation-and-collaboration(5de385a5-e530-49c2-b9a0-bf016df0e554)/export.html.

González, Gloriana, and Anna F. DeJarnette. 2013. "Geometric Reasoning About a Circle Problem." *The Mathematics Teacher* 106 (8): 586–591.doi:10.5951/mathteacher.106.8.0586.

Graves, Elizabeth A. 2008. "Is Role-Playing an Effective Teaching Method?" Unpublished master's thesis. Ohio University.

Gredler, Margaret E., and David H. Jonassen, eds. 2004. "Games and Simulations and Their Relationships to Learning." In *Handbook of Research on Educational Communications and Technology*, 2nd ed., ed. Margaret E. Gredler and David H. Jonassen, 571–581. Mahwah, NJ: Lawrence Erlbaum Associates.

Hake, Richard R. 1998. "Interactive-Engagement Versus Traditional Methods: A Six-Thousand-Student Survey of Mechanics Test Data for Introductory Physics Courses." *American Journal of Physics* 66 (1): 64. doi:10.1119/1.18809.

Herreid, Clyde Freedman. 2005. "Using Case Studies to Teach Science." ActionBioscience. http://www.actionbioscience.org/education/herreid.html.

High School Economics. 2014. 3rd ed. New York: Council for Economic Education.

Hokanson, Brad, and Robert Fraher. 2008. "Narrative Structure, Myth and Cognition for Instructional Design." *Educational Technology* January/February: 27–31.

Honey, Margaret, and Margaret L. Hilton. 2011. *Learning Science Through Computer Games and Simulations*. Washington, DC: National Academies Press.

Isgitt, Jennifer, and Quentin Donnellan. 2014. "Discussion-Based Problem Solving: An English-Calculus Collaboration Emphasizes Cross-Curricular Thinking Skills." *English Journal* 103.3 (January): 80–86.

Jonassen, David H., and Woel Hung. 2008. "All Problems Are Not Equal: Implications for Problem-Based Learning." *Interdisciplinary Journal of Problem-Based Learning* 2 (2): 6–28. http://dx.doi.org/10.7771/1541-5015.1080.

Kane, Thomas, and Douglas Staiger. 2012. "Gathering Feedback for Teaching: Combining High-Quality Observations with Student Surveys and Achievement Gains." Bill & Melinda Gates Foundation. Retrieved from http://www. metproject. org.

Kantrov, Ilene. 2015. "New CTE Model Is a Plus for Schools and Students." *Phi Delta Kappan* 96 (6): 27–32. doi:10.1177/0031721715575296.

Karpiak, Irene E. 2013. "The Weir: Storytelling That Transforms." *Canadian Journal of University Continuing Education CJUCE* 34 (1): 81–94. http://dx.doi. org/10.21225/d5dw2j.

Kaya, Osman Nafiz, and Jazlin Ebenezer. 2007. *High School Students' Affective Dispositions in Science: Scientific Inquiry with Information Technologies.* Presented at American Educational Research Annual Meeting, 2007. https://eric.ed.gov-/?id=ED500737.

King, M. Bruce, Fred M. Newmann, and Dana L. Carmichael. 2009. "Authentic Intellectual Work: Common Standards for Teaching Social Studies." *Social Education* 73 (1): 43–49.

Kipp-Newbold, Rebecca. 2010. "That's Fierce! Collaboration in the English Classroom." *The English Journal* 99 (5): 74–78. http://www.jstor.org/ stable/10.2307/27807196?ref=search-gateway:b4e46a3a5b523470a3f8d-f80c0adc2e3.

Koerth-Baker, Maggie. 2016. "Boredom Gets Interesting." *Nature* 529 (January 14): 146–148.

Kohn, Alfie. 1986. *No Contest: The Case Against Competition.* Boston: Houghton Mifflin.

———. 1987. "The Case Against Competition." *Working Mother* (September). http:// www.alfiekohn.org/article/case-competition/.

Kosa, Jaymie Reeber. 2008. "Tell a Story." *Education Digest: Essential Readings Condensed for Quick Review* 74 (2): 43–47. http://eric.ed.gov/?id=EJ888594.

Ledford, Heidi. 2014. "We Dislike Being Alone with Our Thoughts." *Nature*, July 03. http://www.nature.com/news/we-dislike-being-alone-with-our-thoughts-1.15508. doi:10.1038/nature.2014.15508.

Lemov, Doug. 2010. *Teach Like a Champion: 49 Techniques That Put Students on the Path to College.* San Francisco: Jossey-Bass.

Lemus, Judith D., Kristina Bishop, and Howard Walters. "Quikscience: Effective Linkage of Competitive, Cooperative, and Service Learning in Science Education." *American Secondary Education* 38 (3): 40–61.

Lin, Alex Romeo, Joshua Fahey Lawrence, and Catherine Elizabeth Snow. 2015. "Teaching Urban Youth About Controversial Issues: Pathways to Becoming Active and Informed Citizens." *Citizenship, Social & Economics Education* 14 (2): 103–119. doi:10.1177/2047173415600606.

Liston, Delores D. 1994. *Storytelling and Narrative: A Neurophilosophical Perspective*. https://eric.ed.gov/?q=ED372092.

Little, Timothy W. 2015. "Effects of Digital Game-Based Learning on Student Engagement and Academic Achievement." Order No. 3721273, Lamar University, Beaumont, Texas. Available from ProQuest Dissertations & Theses A&I. (1727140644).

Mac Iver, Martha Abele, and Douglas J. Mac Iver. 2014. *If We Build It, We Will Come: Impacts of a Summer Robotics Program on Regular Year Attendance in Middle School*. Issue brief. Baltimore: BERC.

Macklem, Gayle. 2015. *Boredom in the Classroom: Addressing Student Motivation, Self-Regulation, and Engagement in Learning*. Cham, Switzerland: Springer International.

Maller, Nicole H. 2013. *Diagnosis for Classroom Success: Making Anatomy and Physiology Come Alive*. Arlington, VA: NSTA Press, National Science Teachers Association.

Matsuda, Noboru, Evelyn Yarzebinski, Victoria Keiser, Rohan Raizada, Gabriel J. Stylianides, and Kenneth R. Koedinger. 2013. "Studying the Effect of a Competitive Game Show in a Learning by Teaching Environment." *International Journal of Artificial Intelligence in Education* 23 (1–4): 1–21. doi:10.1007/s40593-013-0009-1.

McAvoy, Paula, and Diana Hess. 2014. "Debates and Conversations: From the Ground Up." *Educational Leadership* (November): 48–53.

McDonald, Jason K. 2009. "Imaginative Instruction: What Master Storytellers Can Teach Instructional Designers." *Educational Media International* 46 (2): 111–122. doi:10.1080/09523980902933318.

Morgan, Wendy, and Glenn Beaumont. 2003. "A Dialogic Approach to Argumentation: Using a Chat Room to Develop Early Adolescent Students' Argumentative Writing." *International Reading Association* 47 (October): 146–157.

Morrison, Judith, Amy Roth Mcduffie, and Brian French. 2015. "Identifying Key Components of Teaching and Learning in a STEM School." *School Science and Mathematics* 115 (5): 244–255. doi:10.1111/ssm.12126.

Nash, Troy R. 2008. "Osmosis Is Serious Business!" National Center for Case Study Teaching in Science, December 15. http://sciencecases.lib.buffalo.edu/cs/collection/detail.asp?case_id=283&id=283.

National Association of Independent Schools (NAIS). 2015. *2014 NAIS Report on the High School Survey of Student Engagement*. Report. Bloomington, IN: NAIS.

Newkirk, Thomas. 2014. *Minds Made for Stories: How We Really Read and Write Informational and Persuasive Texts*. Portsmouth, NH: Heinemann.

Oakes, Jeannie. 1986. "Keeping Track, Part 1: The Policy and Practice of Curriculum Inequality." *Phi Delta Kappan* 68 (1): 12. https://eric.ed.gov/?id=EJ341127.

Ozturk, Elif, and Ucus, Sukran. 2015. "Nature of Science Lessons, Argumentation and Scientific Discussions Among Students in Science Cass: A Case Study in a Successful School." *Journal of Education in Science, Environment and Health (JESEH)* 1 (2): 102–110.

Perkins, David N. 2008. *Making Learning Whole: How Seven Principles of Teaching Can Transform Education*. San Francisco, CA: Jossey-Bass.

Petermann, Kassie. 2016. "Irondale Robotics Team Heading to World Championship." *Sun Focus*, March 27. http://focus.mnsun.com/2016/03/27/irondale-robotics-team-heading-to-world-championship/.

Pimentel, Diane Silva. 2012. "Secondary Science Teachers' and Students' Beliefs About Engaging in Whole-Class Discussions." PhD diss., Boston College. https://dlib.bc.edu/islandora/object/bc-ir:101879/datastream/PDF/view.

Pink, Daniel H. 2012. *Drive: The Surprising Truth About What Motivates Us*. New York: Riverhead Books.

Porter, Bernajean. 2016. "Applied Storytelling: Whoever Tells the Best Stories Rules the World." Lecture, JourneyEd Midwest Conference, Roseville, MN, October 5.

Reeve, Johnmarshall, and Edward L. Deci. 1996. "Elements of the Competitive Situation That Affect Intrinsic Motivation." *Personality and Social Psychology Bulletin* 22 (1): 24–33. doi:10.1177/0146167296221003.

Reeve, Johnmarshall, Bradley C. Olson, and Steven G. Cole. 1985. "Motivation and Performance: Two Consequences of Winning and Losing in Competition." *Motivation and Emotion* 9 (3): 291–298. doi:10.1007/bf00991833.

Ridlon, Candice L. 2009. "Learning Mathematics via a Problem-Centered Approach: A Two-Year Study." *Mathematical Thinking and Learning* 11 (4): 188–225. doi:10.1080/10986060903225614.

Roehling, Patricia Vincent, Thomas Lee Vander Kooi, Stephanie Dykema, Brooke Quisenberry, and Chelsea Vandlen. 2010. "Engaging the Millennial Generation in Class Discussions." *College Teaching* 59 (1): 1–6. doi:10.1080/87567555.2010.484035.

Roney, Craig. 1996. "Storytelling in the Classroom: Some Theoretical Thoughts." *Storytelling World* 9: 7–9.

Ruenzel, David. 2002. "Making Themselves Heard." *Teacher Magazine* 13(7): 24–30. ERIC.

Savery, John R. 2006. "Overview of Problem-Based Learning: Definitions and Distinctions." *Interdisciplinary Journal of Problem-Based Learning* 1 (1): 9–20. http://dx.doi.org/10.7771/1541-5015.1002.

Saye, John, and Social Studies Inquiry Research Collaborative. 2013. "Authentic Pedagogy: Its Presence in Social Studies Classrooms and Relationship to Student Performance on State-Mandated Tests." *Theory & Research in Social Education* 41 (1): 89–132. doi:10.1080/00933104.2013.756785.

Schank, Roger C., and Robert P. Abelson. 1995. "Knowledge and Memory: The Real Story." In *Knowledge and Memory: The Real Story*, ed. Robert S. Wyer, Jr. Hillsdale, NJ: Lawrence Erlbaum Associates, 1–85. http://cogprints.org/636/1/KnowledgeMemory_SchankAbelson_d.html.

Schwartz, Daniel L., and John D. Bransford. 1998. "A Time for Telling." *Cognition and Instruction* 16 (4): 475–522. http://eric.ed.gov/?id=EJ582423.

Schettino, Carmel. 2016. "Aspects of Problem-Based Teaching." NCTM blog entry, September 26. nctm.org. http://www.nctm.org/Publications/Mathematics-Teacher/Blog/Aspects-of-Problem-Based-Teaching/.

Shuster, Kate. 2009. "Civil Discourse in the Classroom." Teaching Tolerance: A Project of the Southern Poverty Law Center. http://www.tolerance.org/sites/default/files/general/TT_Civil%20Discourse_whtppr_0.pdf.

Snyder, Kristen M., and Karen Cooper. 2015. "Innovating Schools Through Dialog Arts-Based Practice: Ingredients for Engaging Students with a Whole New Mind." *Journal for Learning Through the Arts* 11 (1): 2–17. http://escholarship.org/uc/item/1vd3k1qh.

Strobel, Johannes, and Angela Van Barneveld. 2009. "When Is PBL More Effective? A Meta-synthesis of Meta-analyses Comparing PBL to Conventional Classrooms." *Interdisciplinary Journal of Problem-Based Learning* 3 (1): 44–58. doi:10.7771/1541-5015.1046.

Stuart, John, and R. J. Rutherford. 1978. "Medical Student Concentration During Lectures." *The Lancet* 312 (8088): 514–516.

Sunyoung, Han, Robert Capraro, and Mary Margaret Capraro. 2015. "How Science, Technology, Engineering, and Mathematics (STEM) Project-Based Learning (PBL) Affects High, Middle, and Low Achievers Differently: The Impact of Student Factors on Achievement." *International Journal of Science and Mathematics Education* 13: 1089–1113.

Tanner, Michael L., and Leah Casados. 1998. "Promoting and Studying Discussions in Math Classes." *Journal of Adolescent and Adult Literacy* 41 (5): 342–350.

Tillotson, Taylor E., and Judith Puncochar. 2014. "Short Duration Campaign Simulation Increases High School Students' Civic Engagement Skills and Knowledge." Roundtable presentation at the American Educational Research Association's 2014 Annual Meeting, Philadelphia, PA.

Toshalis, Eric. 2015. *Make Me! Understanding and Engaging Student Resistance in School.* Cambridge, MA: Harvard Education Press.

Tze, Virginia M. C., Lia M. Daniels, and Robert M. Klassen. 2016. "Evaluating the Relationship Between Boredom and Academic Outcomes: A Meta-analysis." *Educational Psychology Review* 28 (1): 119–144.

Vansteenkiste, Maarten, and Edward L. Deci. 2003. "Competitively Contingent Rewards and Intrinsic Motivation: Can Losers Remain Motivated?" *Motivation and Emotion* 27 (4): 273–299.

Villar, Luis et al. 2015. "Efficacy of a Tetravalent Dengue Vaccine in Children in Latin America." *New England Journal of Medicine* 372 (2): 113–123. doi:10.1045/nejmoa1411037.

Werhan, Carol R. 2006. "Family and Consumer Sciences Secondary School Programs: National Survey Shows Continued Demand for FCS Teachers." *Journal of Family & Consumer Sciences* 98 (1): 19–25.

Wiggins, Grant. 2009. "Real-World Writing: Making Audience and Purpose Matter." *English Journal* 98 (5): 29–37. http://www.ncte.org/library/NCTEFiles/Resources/Journals/EJ/0985-may09/EJ0985Focus.pdf.

———. 2014. "Fixing the High School—Student Survey, Part 1." *Granted, and . . . Thoughts on Education.* Blog entry, May 21. https://grantwiggins.wordpress.com/2014/05/21/fixing-the-high-school/.

Wilson, Edward O. 2002. "The Power of Story." *American Educator* (Spring): 8–11.

Wong, Kenson Kin Hang, and Jeffrey Richard Day. 2008. "A Comparative Study of Problem-Based and Lecture-Based Learning in Junior Secondary School Science." *Research in Science Education* 39 (5): 625–42. doi:10.1007/s11165-008-9096-7.

Zusak, Markus. 2007. *The Book Thief.* New York: Alfred A. Knopf.

INDEX

Page numbers followed by *f* indicate figures.